Fathers and Sons, Volume 2

"What does it mean to be a real man? Douglas Bond answers this question with clarity, humility, and wisdom. He calls sons and fathers to grow up and be men. This book is a handbook for fathers who earnestly desire to equip their sons to be men of God, men of integrity, and men of humility, relying on God's grace and living for God's glory."

—Burk Parsons, editor, *Tabletalk* magazine; minister, Saint Andrew's Chapel, Sanford, Florida

"Already well established in historical fiction for young people, Douglas Bond now offers a more direct and vital message for young men and their fathers. With ample storytelling ability, he warns them of the pitfalls and opportunities for youth in a debased culture. The result is a first-class textbook on modern culture, with much wise and challenging counsel for young men and their fathers."

—Russ Pulliam, *The Indianapolis Star*

"In a fresh way, *HOLD FAST In a Broken World* covers the waterfront of issues that young men must consider as they ponder the challenges of Christian manhood. Christian fathers need to be great leaders and Christian sons need to study leadership and see leadership modeled for them by their fathers. Douglas Bond has given us a book that will help do that."

—Bentley B. Rayburn, United States Air Force Major General (retired)

"Douglas Bond doesn't write for the faint-hearted. This is for men who want the next generation—including their very own sons—to be more stalwart than they were themselves. . . . Douglas Bond calls you to set your plow shares deep, do the hard work of parenting while it is yet day, and look to a faithful heavenly Father for a rewarding harvest."

—Joel Belz, founder, *World* magazine

"Douglas Bond has a passion for fathers and sons to connect in significant ways, because the truths of Scripture are too important not to pass on. In this second book focused on fathers and sons, Bond clearly and winsomely provides an outline of topics for fathers to share with their sons. Fathers, here is a volume that you can use to direct and deepen your sons to face real life issues, and do it with confidence and grace."

—Dominic A. Aquila, president, New Geneva Seminary,
Colorado Springs

"Fathers, get these books, sit down with your son, pray, and get started. Your son will understand the engaging language and powerful illustrations; you will be thanking God for the help in talking about so many topics you know will benefit your son as he reaches for manhood. Very edifying; don't miss out on this!"

—Paul Walker, pastor and hospital chaplain
(retired), Vancouver, BC

"Full of lively illustrations, wise warnings, and hard-hitting application for everyday life, Bond's latest book addresses all of the strong temptations and difficult trials that young men face today. Ideal for personal study or father-son discussion, *Fathers and Sons* is an invitation to pursue manly godliness in the adventure of life."

—Philip Graham Ryken, senior minister,
Tenth Presbyterian Church, Philadelphia

Fathers and Sons, Volume 2

Hold Fast in a Broken World

Douglas Bond

P U B L I S H I N G
P.O. BOX 817 • PHILLIPSBURG • NEW JERSEY 08865-0817

Printed in the United States of America

Library of Congress Cataloging-in-Publication Data

Bond, Douglas, 1958-
Fathers and sons / Douglas Bond.
  p. cm.
Includes bibliographical references.
ISBN 978-1-59638-076-9 (v. 1: pbk.)
ISBN 978-1-59638-077-6 (v. 2: pbk.)
1. Teenage boys—Religious life. 2. Teenage boys—Conduct of life. 3. Conduct of life—Biblical teaching. 4. Christian life—Biblical teaching. I. Title.
BV4541.3.B65 2007
248.8'32—dc22
2007030982

In Grateful Memory of
My Father,
Douglas Elwood Bond
September 21, 1933–June 12, 2006
"Serve the Lord with Gladness"

For my sons
Rhodri, Cedric, Desmond, Giles

and for the sons that my daughters,
Brittany and Gillian,
God willing, will someday marry

"For we have become partakers of Christ, if we hold fast the beginning of our assurance firm until the end."

Hebrews 3:14 (NASB)

"Hold fast Christ without wavering and contend for the faith, because Christ is not easily gotten nor kept. It is Christianity, my heart, to be sincere, unfeigned, honest and upright hearted before God, and to live and serve God."

Samuel Rutherford, to John Clark, 1637

CONTENTS

YOUNG MEN: LEADERS AND SERVANTS

1

LEARN TO STAND AND HOLD FAST

Hebrews 3:6, 14

Off the Track

Seth, a downhill skier, told me about a race in college where he found himself, at the last minute, requisitioned to fill in for an injured Nordic ski racer.

"I was a pretty good downhill skier," he told me, "but I'd never cross-country-skied in my life." But he was nineteen and invincible. "How hard could cross-country skiing be?" he thought as he latched on the narrow skis. The Nordic 10K freestyle race was the last event of the day, and the winning skier would cross the finish line in around fifteen minutes.

Seth figured that he'd show these weenie Nordic skiers a thing or two about real skiing. But a fraction of a second after the start gun, he began to realize that he might have miscalculated. Lean, spandex-clad Nordic skiers skated off the start, leaving Seth in a heap. But he was a competitor and staggered to his feet, lurching after them as he tried to imitate their powerful stride—a thing growing rapidly more difficult as they disappeared in front of him.

"10K of this?" he thought.

The last skier of the pack crossed the finish line half an hour later, but there was no sign of Seth. Granted, it was getting hard to see; night falls rapidly in the Cascade Mountains in winter. Forty-five minutes— still no Seth. Now it was fully dark.

Hopelessly far behind the other skiers, Seth had gotten off the track. Alone, he'd lost his way in the darkness. He spent the next two and a half hours staggering around in the cold and snow, trying to make his way back to the start line. He's never been cross-country skiing since.

The race of life has a particularly "icy, slippery way," in it called *youth*. Don't underestimate the difficulties. Add cultural enticements lying in wait around every corner, and youth becomes a skid road to disaster. Therefore, you must learn to hold fast, or you will lose your way.

Truth

War correspondent Stephen Crane wrote a perceptive verse about life that begins, "The wayfarer, perceiving the pathway to truth." Though he perceives the pathway, he immediately faces an obstacle. The path to truth was "thickly grown with weeds"; few travelers were going to the trouble to take that road. Little wonder. It's a pathway that looks painful, one that is sure to be hard on the feet. At the last, Crane's persona concludes, "Doubtless there are other roads."

The world offers you a smorgasbord approach to life. Blaring at you from every pop-cultural signpost are messages urging you to find your own path, to make your own way in the world, to take one of the "other roads." But there's a problem. "To live after the course of the world," wrote Samuel Rutherford in a letter to Ninian Mure, a young Scottish man, "will not bring you to heaven."

The path of truth is singular; it is absolutely exclusive. And yes, Crane was right; the pathway to truth can be hard on the feet. But only one pathway leads to heaven. So how does a young man stay in that way; how does he hold fast to his course when the path is littered with sharp obstacles?

By taking heed to the Word of God. Young men who know the truth, who are determined to hold fast to truth, to stay in the pathway, must be daily students of the divine travel guide, the Bible, the only perfectly reliable guidebook, devoid of error.

The "other roads" require you to stop thinking. But the Word and the Spirit renew your fallen reason, so that by God's grace you can think aright. A young man who stands fast for truth, who holds fast against error, must become a skillful thinker. He must cultivate sanctified thoughts, thoughts reined in and kept on a leash, thoughts full of awe and wonder at Christ.

And he will do this early. "I entreat you," wrote Rutherford, "now in the morning of your life, seek the Lord and his face." Wise young men seek early, like King Uzziah, who learned the fear of the Lord as a boy. Then, as a sixteen-year-old king, "he did what was right in the eyes of the LORD" (2 Chron. 26:4).

Pride

Until he became proud. It was Uzziah's undoing, and it will be yours, if you don't hold fast to humility. Pride always has gone and always will go before a fall, yet so few young men take the crushingly destructive power of pride seriously.

I was reminded of just how early pride sets its hook in young men while reading about the latest golf prodigy, Reese Matthew Campbell Murphy, from Newmills, Scotland. Hold this kid's childhood golf record up next to Tiger Woods's, and he's impressive, including not one, but two holes in one so far. In an interview, he was asked whether he wanted to be a great golfer someday. He looked askance at the reporter and replied in his baby brogue, "I'm already a great golfer."

He's only six years old!

Many things fuel men's pride, but sports ranks highest for most young men. You want to win. You want to be the greatest. You want to run the fastest, jump the highest, hit the hardest. You want to crush your opponent, and get all the credit for doing it. All this is pride, and though the Scriptures clearly warn us that God resists the proud man but gives grace to the humble man, we persist in our pride.

With athletics, you can easily find yourself running the wrong race. Instead of fixing your eyes on Jesus, instead of straining every spiritual muscle on the course of truth and life, the only path that leads to heaven, you can easily sell your soul to the god of the gridiron, the almighty of athletics. You must beware of pride. You must put it to death. By the grace of God, you must do it now.

Idols

Men are "idol-making factories," John Calvin termed us, and one of the greatest idols that men create for themselves in the modern world is money. "Money! Nothing worse in our lives, so current, so rampant, so corrupting." Come to think of it, maybe it's not just modern man's problem. Sophocles, the paragon of Greek tragedy, penned these words twenty-five hundred years ago: "Money—you demolish cities, root men from their homes; you train and twist good minds and set them on to the most atrocious schemes. No limit, you make them adept at every kind of outrage, every godless crime—money!"

Christian young men must beware of the love of money, of worshiping at the shrine of wealth, of pitching their hopes on material prosperity—and so forfeiting their souls. Sell your soul for thirty pieces of silver or thirty million pieces, it makes no difference in hell.

There are other kinds of idols, ones of the heart and imagination. Lustful thoughts after the body of an attractive young woman become a form—a highly destructive form—of idolatry. You live in a pornographic world, a world that wears itself out making sin look appealing. The devil "will paint, and mask, and dress up sin," wrote J. C. Ryle, "in order to make you fall in love with it. He will exalt the pleasure of wickedness, but he will keep out of sight the sting." Men slain by sexual sin are a vast and miserable host.

But you may be operating under the delusion that you can keep sexual sins secret, just between you and your imagination. It's a lie, one that will be exposed for all to see, to your undying shame, on the judgment day. Others may never know your secret sins, but before God's eye every thought, every desire is laid bare.

"I lived according to my desires," said Rich Young, former lead guitarist with heavy-metal band Lucian Blaque. He admits that his former life was full of "sexual immorality, lust, profanity, drunkenness, and wild parties." Of his rock and roll, he said, "I used to make music for me." Then Christ wonderfully saved Rich. And for ten years he wouldn't touch a guitar because he suddenly understood something about his music: "I wrote music so people would get physical."

A young man who cares about his soul will not delude himself into thinking that the music he listens to has no effect on him. What you listen to profoundly affects your desires for, your thoughts about, and your treatment of women. A man who cares about his soul knows that the kind of music he listens to directly affects his ability to exercise self-control.

Self-control

"Beware of the folly of dangerous youth," wrote Rutherford, "a perilous time for your soul." Young men have the ruinous inequity of strength disproportionate to their wisdom. So keeping your way pure, holding fast against the enemies of your soul, demands a virulent self-control. Rutherford offered a strategy to help young men with self-control: "Love not the world; keep faith and truth; walk with God, for he seeth you; prize Christ and salvation above all the world."

Self-controlled young men have sanctified affections. They love what they should love; they walk by faith informed by truth; they live for an audience of one—God; they value Christ and his salvation more than all the allurements of the world.

Self-controlled young men take sin seriously. They don't see how close to the edge of the cliff they can cavort. They're aware that the devil and sin are nothing to flirt with. They avoid sin, its occasions, and its companions because they know how devious the devil can be.

German writer Heinrich Heine explored this in a poem that begins, "I called the devil and he came." But he didn't have horns and a flame-red jumpsuit like cartoonist Gary Larsen's devil always has. "He was not hideous . . . / But a genial man with charming ways." Wise young men don't flirt with the devil and sin because they know that the devil will outwit them. He's called the deceiver for a reason. Therefore, wise young men know they must be self-controlled, or they will be devil-controlled.

But it's not only the devil. It's a three-way conspiracy, with the world and your own flesh joining eagerly to secure your soul for hell. They conspire to normalize sin and earthly things so that you, at the last, lose all appetite for heaven. They want righteousness to seem odd and sin to seem normal to you. "We children think the earth a fair garden," wrote Rutherford. "It is but God's out-field, and wild, cold, barren ground; all things are fading that are here."

But it doesn't seem that way to young men bombarded by an alluring popular culture. You can begin to long for what appears to be the "fair garden" of this world. And you can scorn the palatial splendor of eternal glory. Many things in this world are designed to thicken the veil, to dull the eyes of your faith, to make the here and now all there is.

Emmanuel's Land

While my family and I enjoyed the sights and events at the Inverary Games in the Scottish Highlands, I heard a local story that illustrates just how switched around young men can get things.

It was an idyllic setting, with Highland fanfare unfolding in the shadow of a fairy-tale castle, the ancient fortress of the dukes of Argyle. Then there were whispers all around. In full tartan regalia, jaunty pheasant feathers in his blue bonnet, the Duke of Argyle appeared. Bagpipes skirled out "Scotland the Brave," as the duke, the host of the Highland games, strode onto the green. Later, I stood but an arm's reach from him.

In this setting we heard a story about the duke told by "Mrs. Nothing," an elderly town gossip who "misses nothing." She lived in the considerably humbler village nearby, made up of closely packed tenement houses, occupied by common folks like herself.

Mrs. Nothing told how as a youth the future duke had come home one day to the splendor of his family castle after attending school in the village. He flung himself into a velvet chair next to a full suit of standing armor, and said, "Why do I have to live in this old castle?" Anyone viewing the scene would have thought he was joking. But he was in earnest. "Why can't I live in a tenement house in the village, like all my friends?"

The devil wants you to value the tenement house of worldly pleasures. He wants you to think that the world is all there is. But the last thing he wants you to see is the splendor of heaven, the glory of Emmanuel's land. He wants to deceive you into trading a grand, heavenly fortress for a broken-down, drafty, low-income hovel. He promises you the world—but gives you nothing. He wants you to trade your heavenly birthright for a bowl of soup. Esau did. Make sure you do not.

Cultural Deep Waters

Christian men are called to be self-controlled leaders in a culture desperate to sever all connection with the Christian past and to silence the moral assumptions that have informed men and leaders for centuries. It's your task in this cultural valley of the shadow of death to reaffirm your role and calling as Christian men, with courage and strength, to lead your culture in the pathway of truth.

Such a calling demands prodigious strength and courage, if you are to prevail. Yours is a culture of death expressed in art and music, and in the legalized slaughter of unborn children by the millions. Yours is a culture that stands in defiance of God's authority and truth, seen in the normalizing of homosexuality and the relentless push to deconstruct marriage. Yours is a culture desperate to legitimize homosexual perversion by passing laws that make same-sex marriage a thing to be celebrated. Yours is a culture systematically redefining words in an effort to silence Christians—especially Christian men.

This volume will take you into the trenches of many of these cultural and cosmic battles raging about you. If you are to survive in such a culture, Christian young man, you must begin training with your weapons now. You are called to hold fast your profession in a dark and sinful world, hell-bent on steering culture and belief as far away from biblical truth as it possibly can. Holding fast to Christ in such a world will not be easy. Some who profess Christ, alas, will slacken their grip, will cave in to the cultural byways, and will prove themselves castaways.

You must know your enemy, know the truth, be unshakably persuaded of it, and equip yourself to live with strength and courage for Christ—even while a hostile world scoffs and scorns.

The Last Battle

And finally, you must prepare yourself for the last battle. These volumes for fathers and sons are dedicated in part to the memory of my father, who died while I was writing them. In that dying, he taught me many things about how to be a man of God when facing the last battle in this life. He taught me things I'm still learning and that I want to teach my four sons: how to live with strength and courage; how to die with strength and courage.

The last and great battle you will face is philosophy's one great problem. You or your father will be called on—and it will take prodigious strength and courage—to lay the other in the grave. It will not always be the son hearing his father's last breath, feeling his hand grow limp and cold, and closing his father's eyes. You will read of the heart-wrenching loss when a father must lay his dear son in the grave.

Strength and courage, skill with your spiritual weapons, standing and holding fast against the enemies of your soul takes practice and training. Strength and courage will not be yours unless you make culti-vating Christlike strength and courage your life's work. Learn strength and courage early, or you may never learn it at all. If you do not, the last battle will be a horrific nightmare, a crushing rout that leaves you in the dark.

Posture

It sounds like the outcome could be a close call. But for the true man of God—victory is certain! Greater is he who is in you than he who is in the world. Victory is certain for the wise young man who plants his feet, squares his spiritual shoulders, and holds fast against the enemies of his soul. By the grace of God, he does this by keeping his back against the world, the flesh, and the devil. He's unimpressed by the world, by its entertainments, by pop culture. He's impervious to its allure, unshakable in his stance against sin and evil.

By filling his mind and heart with the Word of truth, he holds this posture against all comers. He has turned his face, as John Bunyan put it, toward the Celestial City. Which means that he has eyes of faith that see Christ, and he lives knowing he is seen by Christ. "If we knew the glory of our elder Brother in heaven," Rutherford wrote, "we should long to be there to see him, and to get our fill of heaven." That's how you hold fast against the cultural slings and arrows designed to destroy you.

In the pages that follow, you will read of ugly and disturbing things—ugly and disturbing because they are produced by a culture that has found the pathway to truth too difficult, too unattractive. It has convinced itself that "doubtless there are other ways." There are, but they all lead to hell. There's but one that leads to Emmanuel's land, to heaven.

The stakes, young man, are high. Plant your feet. Hold fast.

Prayer Resolves

- To take sin seriously
- To know the devil's schemes and resist him, the world, and my own flesh
- To keep my eyes on heaven

Scripture Memory

"For we have become partakers of Christ, if we hold fast the beginning of our assurance firm until the end."

Hebrews 3:14 (NASB)

For Discussion

1. In what ways do you value worldly things over heavenly ones?
2. How can you use your strength for others by developing leadership skills?

"Fight the Good Fight"

Fight the good fight with all thy might;
Christ is thy strength, and Christ thy right:
Lay hold on life, and it shall be
Thy joy and crown eternally.

John S. B. Monsell, 1863

For Further Study

1 Timothy 6:12; Psalm 1

2

LEARN TO WORSHIP

Isaiah 58:13–14

"Place of Worship"

The start gun cracked, and in a flurry of churning water, they were off. Peter's boat rocketed into the lead like a torpedo launched out of an attack submarine. I inwardly hoped that this kid wouldn't beat my son too badly.

It was the 500-meter final on the Cedar River, the last race of day one in a Saturday/Sunday regatta. There were two boats to watch: Peter's and my eldest son Rhodri's. To be honest, I was not hopeful for my son. Peter had been paddling fully two years longer and was in the division above Rhodri. What's more, he was at least a year and a half older, with bulging gymnast muscles to prove it. I began planning how I might help Rhodri learn character from losing this race.

Then, within meters of the finish, a strange thing occurred. Rhodri seemed to tap in to another source of power. I couldn't believe what

I was seeing. My wife screamed and dug her fingernails into my arm. Within three or four strokes of the finish, Rhodri's boat had overtaken Peter's by inches. When the froth settled, my son had widened the gap to a definitive victory.

Peter was not accustomed to losing. In his division, he would go on to be the fastest paddler in the USA. Nor was Peter's coach very happy. As the young men paddled up to the float, I overheard an interchange between Peter and his coach.

"So what happened?" the coach demanded.

Peter shrugged and said nothing.

"You'd better change things around tomorrow," the coach said.

Peter seemed to brighten. "I will," he said with confidence.

"Why so sure?"

Peter tossed a look at Rhodri, and said, "Place of worship."

Word travels fast. Peter wasn't worried about losing to Rhodri on Sunday because he knew that Rhodri wouldn't be paddling on Sunday. It seemed curious the way the young man said it: "Place of worship." As if to say, Rhodri won't be racing because the place of worship was higher on his priorities than paddling.

Sabbath Paddling

Sprint canoe and kayak racing in the United States is a fairly unknown sport. Though it's wildly popular in other parts of the world, especially Eastern Europe, and is the fourth largest Olympic sport, mention two-time Olympic gold-medalist sprint kayak racer Greg Barton to your average American sports fan and all you'll get is, "Huh?"

One thing is clear. Sports has become so important in our society that virtually no one thinks twice about major sporting events happening on Sunday.

Before my sons became serious about kayak racing, I knew I needed to have a heart-to-heart with the coach. I explained to him that we are Christians who take the Lord's Day seriously, that what we do on his day is a measure of what is most important in all of life. I then went on to explain that kayak racing, fun as it is, would never rank as high or higher than the worship of God on the Lord's Day. In short, we were not going to participate in regattas on Sundays.

He was okay with that, because U.S. nationals did not typically include Sunday racing, and there were only a handful of regional races that were both Saturday and Sunday. So we jumped into the sport with vigor and enthusiasm. My sons had grown up sailing and rowing boats and with good water savvy, so they rapidly developed their skills. Since that Saturday race on the Cedar River, my two eldest sons have managed to work their way to the top tier of national competition.

Never Heard of That

Then came an opportunity of a lifetime. Both Rhodri and his younger brother Cedric had won slots to compete in the West Coast team trials at the Olympic Training Center in San Diego. They were thrilled. So was I. Until I asked their coach what the schedule was.

"Heats on Friday, semifinals on Saturday, and finals on . . ."—he paused—". . . on Sunday."

He knew what I would say.

"I'll see what I can do," he said.

The next day he was on the phone with the U.S. Olympic coach, who would be at the trials minutely studying each paddler. Our coach was convinced that a great deal depended on the outcome of these trials. They talked for two and a half hours. The boys' coach reported to me that when he tried to explain to the Olympic coach that my boys wouldn't paddle on Sunday, he replied, "Never heard of that."

A couple of weeks passed, in which my sons and I prayed about all this and committed our way to the Lord. But we agreed. They wouldn't be paddling on Sunday. However well they placed in heats and semifinals, the finals were scheduled for Sunday; if the boys didn't race on Sunday, they would gain no points for the entire trials. Humanly speaking, for kayak racing, they were forfeiting the chance of a lifetime.

25

Then the phone rang. "I just got a call from the Olympic paddling coach." The boys' coach was breathless. "He's switched everything around. They're doing heats, semis, and finals on Friday and Saturday. No Sunday racing agenda. He did it just so the Bond boys could race."

O me of little faith. I couldn't believe it. Both of my sons managed to qualify in these trials, and one of them went on to represent the U.S. national team in the Czech Republic at Junior Worlds, an essential step before making the U.S. Olympic team. We'll have to see what's next.

My boys and I gave thanks to God. We discussed how God didn't always choose to work things out like this, but come what may, obeying the Lord and keeping his day holy was always right, whatever temporal opportunities must be forfeited. "He who honors me, him will I honor."

Not for Us

When it comes to the Sabbath, most Americans would agree with the U.S. Olympic paddling coach: "Never heard of that before." To a non-Christian, the idea of setting one day in seven apart for worship, fellowship, family time, and feasting makes no sense. Give up overtime pay at work? Miss the big game on TV? Deprive yourself of a trip to the beach on a warm summer day? Miss the big sale at the mall? All for some archaic notion of keeping the Sabbath? No thanks.

But it's not just non-Christians who think this way. Most post-conservative evangelicals think pretty much like the world about what pleases God on Sunday. Many will even argue that keeping the Sabbath is pharisaic legalism. All that passed away with the Old Testament. We're not under Jewish law but under grace, they'll insist, as they lace up their cleats and load the kids into the SUV and head off to the soccer field—on Sunday. Or off to the dog show, or beach, or mall—or boat race. "Sabbath-keeping is not for us," most Christians say, then in the same breath, "Hey, check out the sale price on these Adidas!"

Christians who care to be biblical have sometimes concluded that they don't have to keep the Sabbath based on a misinterpretation of Colossians 2:16: "Therefore do not let anyone judge you by what you eat or drink, or with regard to a religious festival, a New Moon celebration or a Sabbath day." Though the text nowhere says that Christians do not need to keep the Sabbath, some have concluded that this text clears away Sabbath-keeping, relegating it to an Old Testament, outmoded, Jewish practice.

But this is a huge interpretive error. Let me illustrate why. Paul is almost quoting from Isaiah 1:13, where the Lord is rebuking his children for heartless Sabbath assembling. "Stop bringing meaningless offerings! Your incense is detestable to me. New Moons, Sabbaths and convocations—I cannot bear your evil assemblies."

Conclude that Paul is abolishing Sabbath-keeping in his epistle to the Colossians, and you must also conclude that the Lord himself is abolishing the Sabbath in Isaiah 1:13. Turn over a few pages in Isaiah, however, and it's abundantly clear that God is doing no such thing:

> If you keep your feet from breaking the Sabbath
>   and from doing as you please on my holy day,
> if you call the Sabbath a delight
>   and the LORD's holy day honorable,
> and if you honor it by not going your own way
>   and not doing as you please or speaking idle words,
> then you will find your joy in the LORD,
>   and I will cause you to ride on the heights of the land
>   and to feast on the inheritance of your father Jacob. (Isa. 58:13–14)

Just as the prophet Isaiah was doing, Paul is reminding first-century Christians that their worship of God must come from the heart; they must mean all that they say and do in the worship of God. Paul is specifically addressing the problem of converts who claimed to hope in Christ but whose real hope was in the extrabiblical Jewish laws about how one observed the Sabbath. Paul is exposing the fraud of all the touch-not, taste-not, handle-not, man-made regulations practiced in first-century Judaism.

When others stand as judges over your Sabbath-keeping, they do their best to make sure that you miss all the delight. Man-made laws become drudgery and are always more about what you cannot do than what you get to do. Thus, Paul tells these Christians not to let anyone judge them by man-made Sabbath regulations. But it makes a mingle-mangle of the Bible's teaching on the Lord's Day to spin Paul into letting us off to do as we please on the Sabbath.

Unlike human regulators of the Sabbath, God ordained one day in seven not to make life miserable for his children. He designed it for our benefit and delight. And it's more delightful to obey and keep his day holy than to shop or go boating or do anything else that rivals worship and fellowship with God and his saints. What we miss when we scorn the Sabbath is the joy of the Lord, riding on the heights of the land, and the delicious feasting on the inheritance of our father Jacob. What could be more delightful!

Which Sabbath?

French philosopher and hater of organized religion Voltaire understood the centrality of the Christian Sabbath. "If you wish to destroy the Christian religion," he said, "you must first destroy the Christian Sunday."

So not only did French Revolutionaries tear down all Christian symbols from churches and cemeteries, and not only did they dub Notre Dame Cathedral in Paris "The Temple of Reason," in their Herculean efforts to expunge every vestige of Christianity from France, they abolished the seven-day week by establishing a calendar with a ten-day week. This was in direct defiance of the God of creation and his Word in Genesis 2:3: "And God blessed the seventh day and made it holy, because on it he rested from all the work of creating that he had done."

But there are those who smugly point out that the Christian Sabbath is not the seventh day. The Sabbath Isaiah was writing about, they quibble, fell on our Saturday, so you're not actually keeping the Sabbath by observing it on Sunday. I can't recollect any of the folks with whom I've had this discussion keeping either day holy, so I'm not so sure they had any practical interest in the outcome of the discussion.

Nevertheless, it's clear in Exodus 20:8–10 that God commands us to "remember the Sabbath day by keeping it holy. Six days you shall labor and do all your work, but the seventh day is a Sabbath to the LORD your God. On it you shall not do any work."

The best answer to this argument comes, again, from the Bible itself. Trace back through the centuries to when the Saturday-to-Sunday shift happened, and you land directly on a number of pages of God's Word. All the gospel writers begin the historical account of the resurrection of our Lord with the phrase "on the first day of the week" (Matt. 28:1; Mark 16:2; Luke 24:1; John 20:1). Collaborate "on the first day of the week," describing when the church gathered in Acts 20:7, 1 Corinthians 11:20 and 16:2, and Revelation 1:10, with the universal practice of the early church down to the present, and you are on safe biblical ground to celebrate the Christian Sabbath on Sunday, the Lord's Day.

Moreover, I'm convinced that the Christian who chooses otherwise has more explaining to do than the one who keeps the Lord's Day holy to the Lord on Sunday. Applying Pascal's Wager to biblical interpretation, I believe that I would have more to answer for if I failed to follow the Christian Sabbath than if I kept the Jewish seventh-day Sabbath. The shift places Christ's resurrection as the central event in the history of redemption, and thus by keeping the Sunday Sabbath we honor Christ our Redeemer in his victory over sin and death.

I suspect that Voltaire intuitively understood this and knew that undermining Sunday Sabbath-keeping was the sure way to destroy true Christianity. About this he was absolutely correct. Unfortunately, most Christians pooh-pooh such a notion, and so unwittingly aid Christian-haters like Voltaire in their scheme to destroy true Christianity.

How Much Will It Cost?

We Americans think in knee-jerk economic terms about most things. "How much will it cost?" we ask about keeping the Sabbath holy unto our Lord. How much did obedience cost our Lord? Especially in our post-Christian world, obedience in Sabbath-keeping will cost you. The young man who takes God's Word seriously about the Sabbath will appear odd and out of step, and it will cost him. But then, all this is true of being a Christian.

Given postconservative evangelicalism's indifference about the Sabbath, it was a wonder that the 1981 film *Chariots of Fire* received such critical acclaim and sweeping popularity. The film pitted two worldviews against each other: Harold Abrahams, a secular Jew who ran to prove something about his own worth to the world, to feel his own pleasure; and Eric Liddell, the Scots Presbyterian missionary's son, the Flying Scotsman. When Liddell ran he felt the Lord's pleasure, and no inducement could dispose him to evoke the Lord's *dis*pleasure—not even if it cost him a gold medal at the 1924 Olympics.

Which it nearly did. Liddell was favored to win the 100-meter sprint, and all Scotland held its breath to see him bring home the first Olympic gold Scotland had ever won. In the movie, as Liddell boarded the steamship for France and the Paris Games, he learned at the last minute that heats for the 100-meter race were scheduled for a Sunday. In fact, the "real" Liddell had known about the Sunday heats for some weeks and had deliberately withdrawn from the event rather than displease God by breaking the Sabbath.

Make no mistake. Liddell was no self-righteous legalist who imagined that he could earn points with God by not running on the Sabbath. People don't admire legalists. He was an earnest young man who believed and did what pleased God—and all the world was watching.

Unyielding in his determination to keep the Christian Sabbath holy, as the Olympics neared, no argument could persuade Liddell to race on the Lord's Day. "I, for one, intend to keep it holy," he said with conviction. So with precious little time, he began training for the 400 meters, a grueling event that he was not favored to win.

But he did. While critics and supporters looked on, Liddell defied the odds and—arms flaying and face lifted heavenward—he won the gold in the 400 meters.

The Lord's Day—A Win-Win

Inexplicably, the world looks on with admiration at Eric Liddell's heroic stand. Why the fascination with Liddell's convictions when so few Christians share them? Perhaps it is that sense that there is something profoundly more important than the world's glitter. Deep down we know that "all that glitters is not gold."

For Christian men, Liddell's stand ought to help us reevaluate our priorities. Is worldly gain more important than obeying Christ, than honoring his name on his day, than finding our delight in worship, prayer, the study of his Word, and the joyful fellowship of the saints around the table of the Lord?

God ordained one day in seven not to make his children miserable. He designed it for our benefit and delight. Liddell concluded that it was more delightful to obey and keep God's day holy than to win an Olympic gold medal.

Every wise young man should scorn anything that rivals worship and fellowship with God and his saints on the Sabbath. Meanwhile, fools will continue to scorn the Sabbath and forfeit the joy of the Lord, riding on the heights of the land, and the delicious feasting on the inheritance of our father Jacob.

Real men who practice the joy of Sabbath-keeping know that obeying God, regardless of the glitter they choose to forgo, is always a win-win situation. Sure, you can become pharisaic about keeping the Sabbath and in so doing fail to love your neighbor as yourself. And when that rare case arises when keeping the Lord's Day holy and loving one's neighbor conflict, God will give light to the young man who truly desires to honor the Lord.

The Christian Sabbath falls on the same day that our Lord triumphantly burst forth from the tomb, and it is the first day that his Father began creating the world with the brilliant declaration: "Let there be light!" Walk in that light every Sabbath of your life, and so honor Christ. "He who honors me, him will I honor."

Prayer Resolves

- To find my delight in the Lord always, and especially on his holy day
- To plan ahead what I will do, what I will read, where I will go, what I will fill my mind and conversation with on the Lord's Day

Scripture Memory

"If you honor [the Sabbath] by not going your own way
     and not doing as you please or speaking idle words,
then you will find your joy in the LORD,
     and I will cause you to ride on the heights of the land
     and to feast on the inheritance of your father Jacob."

Isaiah 58:13–14

For Discussion

1. Read Westminster Shorter Catechism questions 59 through 62.
2. Discuss these alongside the biblical texts for further study below.

"This Day at Thy Creating Word"

O day of light and life and grace,
From earthly toil sweet resting place,
Thy hallowed hours, blest gift of love,
Give we again to God above.

William Walsham How, 1871

For Further Study

Acts 20:7; 1 Corinthians 11:20; 16:2; Revelation 1:10

3

LEARN FREEDOM

Galatians 5:1, 13–14; 1 Corinthians 8:9–13; 9:19–23

Watts and Freedom

The winter of 1780, the coldest winter recorded in the entire eighteenth century, wreaked havoc on American morale. George Washington's army dwindled as men starved and froze to death—some resorted to desertion. The cause of American independence teetered more precariously on the verge of disaster than at any other stage of the war.

With six thousand fresh troops, the British decided to make a final push from New York to invade New Jersey and thereby decisively end the war. Meanwhile, after rallying the beleaguered New Jersey Brigade and the local militia, General "Scotch Willie" Maxwell found himself in command of a ragtag army totaling no more than two thousand men.

Though outnumbered three to one, General "Scotch Willie" ordered a bayonet charge that sent the British advance guard hightailing it back to their main force. The militia harried the flank of the advancing British army with musket fire, striking hard, then disappearing to fire on the opposite flank, leaving many redcoat casualties behind.

During the fighting, Tories opened fire on a house where Hannah Caldwell, wife of Presbyterian parson James Caldwell, comforted her children in the smoke and confusion of the battle. Caldwell's wife was shot and killed, and the village was burned to the ground by the British.

Pastor Caldwell, graduate of Princeton, fervent Christian, zealous pastor, and intrepid patriot, tirelessly served as both militia chaplain and—after the British shot his wife—combatant. On June 23, 1780, at the decisive Battle of Springfield, when the British made their final desperate push to regain New Jersey, the American troops found themselves completely out of wadding to load their muskets. Caldwell ran to the local Presbyterian church and snatched up an armload of hymnals. "Put Watts into 'em, Boys!" he cried as he dispensed the wadding to the militia.

No doubt Caldwell believed there were better uses for Isaac Watts's hymns; nevertheless, these were desperate times. The British withdrew from New Jersey and never came back. Speaking to Congress, George Washington said of the men who fought at Springfield, "The militia deserves everything that can be said. They flew to arms universally, and acted with a spirit equal to anything I have seen in the course of the war."

Later shot by a sentinel, Pastor Caldwell was buried next to his wife in Elizabethtown, New Jersey. "His name will be cherished," his monument reads, "in the Church and in the State so long as virtue is esteemed, and patriotism honored."

Freedom by Design

Political freedom runs hot in the veins of most people living in our democratic age. Combine your American heritage, however, with coming-of-age teenaged male love of independence, and you've got the potential for a powder keg of problems.

You want to make your own decisions, and you're confident that you're capable of making them. Your dad doesn't agree. In fact, at times, he's absolutely certain that you're not ready. I suspect that most of your conflicts with him come as you clash over freedom. You want the car keys. He won't let you have them. What's the problem here?

Part of the problem lies in defining words. You are sure that *freedom* means making your own decisions and doing whatever you would like to do. Your dad's definition is a bit different.

He's thinking that bank robbers do whatever they want; axe murderers do whatever they want; sexual perverts do whatever they want. All of these got their start by thinking that freedom meant doing whatever they wanted. It's what young men naturally conclude. Your dad himself probably remembers feeling this way when he was a kid.

But now he knows better. Wise fathers understand that the end result of acting on your desires is anything but freedom. A wise father thinks of freedom more the way the Bible commentator Matthew Henry expressed it: "A man is free not when he can do what he wishes to do but when he wishes to do, and can do, what he ought to do."

We were made in the image of God, made to love him, to know him, and to do his will. Why did Christ say that his yoke is easy and his burden is light? Because following Christ means obeying and living life according to design. God designed you to find joy and satisfaction by conforming to his will. Thus, Matthew Henry got it right when he concluded that a man is free only after the Spirit of God changes his desires and gives him the ability to do what he ought to do, what he was designed to do.

Real freedom comes when you desire to do and are doing what you were made to do—to glorify and enjoy God, now and forever.

Self-control and Freedom

Why does Paul tell us to "be careful" in the exercise of our freedom (1 Cor. 8:9)? He knows something about men. Liberty easily devolves into a swaggering license to sin. And thus, we must be careful with liberty. Our practice of freedom must be regulated by inward self-control, guided by love for God and our neighbor—something that most men have far too little of.

While lead was flying at the Battle of Springfield, British parliamentarian Edmund Burke made an astute observation about men and freedom:

> Men qualify for freedom in exact proportion to their disposition to put moral chains on their own appetites. Society cannot exist unless a controlling power is put somewhere on will and appetite, and the less of it there is within, the more of it there must be without. It is ordained in the eternal constitution of things that men of intemperate minds cannot be free. Their passions forge their fetters.

God looks on the heart—within us where all freewheeling sin originates. Burke observed that free men are free because an internal "controlling power" has placed "moral chains" deep within a man. Thus, freedom, ironically, comes from submission to moral boundaries. Put simply, self-control brings freedom. Correspondingly, passion, or the absence of moral restraint on one's desires, enslaves a man.

Many things are counterintuitive about life in a fallen world. It seems as though freedom ought to be the absence of restraint, no rules, just do your own thing. Postmodernity insists that there is no absolute truth; thus, men are free to throw off outmoded rules and live as they desire—a soul-killing, anarchist's worldview, one that inevitably destroys civilization. Freedom thus conceived, however, destroys because it doesn't fit with the design. For society as for the individual, freedom must be informed and regulated by truth—or you lose it.

Truth and Freedom

Whether it's the gridiron or the guitar, you will never achieve freedom without conforming to the rules. Watch the precision as a quarterback makes that perfect pass, the fleet-footed wide receiver leaping at precisely the right second and catching the football in the end zone. They didn't get there by doing their own thing.

Listen to Christopher Parkening play J. S. Bach on the classical guitar, and you will hear a musician who effortlessly does whatever he pleases with the guitar strings, making music that anoints listeners and holds them spellbound with that mysterious power of music. He got there by a lifetime of playing by the rules.

Likewise, freedom in any other discipline comes not from doing as you please, but from submitting to the rules, mastering them, and thereby achieving real freedom. To be free in anything, you must play by the rules "ordained in the eternal constitution of things," as Burke put it.

"You will know the truth," Christ put it, "and the truth will set you free" (John 8:32). Knowing truth means that you live your life in fear of God, before his face, acknowledging his authority over your life, acknowledging his love and care expressed in his commands.

Learn self-control and you will gain skill. Learn self-control and you will become a master at whatever your hand finds to do. Learn self-control and your dad will gladly give you more and more freedom. I guarantee it.

Sixteenth-century poet and knight extraordinaire Sir Phillip Sidney understood self-control. He understood that mastery comes for the man who "humble[s] all [his] might to that sweet yoke where lasting freedoms be." Being self-controlled means aspiring to higher things, humbly bowing under the Lord's authority, cheerfully and wholeheartedly submitting to his rule. Sidney knew, as did Welsh poet Anna Waring, that "a life of self-renouncing love is one of liberty."

Christian Liberty

"Glorious freedom" does await the children of God (Rom. 8:21), and we are called to freedom. But we can so easily use our "freedom to indulge the sinful nature" (Gal. 5:13). Many postconservative Christians set about discovering their liberties as if Paul had never made such a caution. We must beware.

With freedom things easily get wrenched out of shape, and "glorious freedom" turns sour and becomes the back door to slavery all over again. Just as American independence from British rule made some men think they determined their own destiny, so Christians easily distort their glorious freedom into a rationale for indulging in worldliness.

Of liberties in Christ, Calvin urged Christians "diligently to guard against turning helps into hindrances." Christian liberty as Paul describes it is supposed to be one of those helps to holiness. Wise Christians must beware of how easily those helps become impenetrable barricades to serious Christian piety.

Growing up in a fundamentalist Baptist home, we didn't talk much about Christian liberty. I've concluded, however, that whatever flaws there were in separatist fundamentalism, suspicion of the corrupting nature of worldly influences was not one of them.

There is a great danger for Christians whose lives become a quest for Christian liberty. At lightning speed, newfound liberties, instead of being an expression of our slavery to Christ, who has set us free from the tyranny of the devil, produce a cavalier and presumptive worldliness.

Instead of liberty to serve and love our neighbor, Christian liberty becomes a list of wicked little worldly things that we're enlightened enough to get to do, while the poor, benighted, ignorant Christians miss out. Absurdly, the practice of pet Christian liberties becomes, for many, the central dogmas of faith, the sacred cows of orthodoxy.

Liberty *from* Depravity

Because of our emphasis on the cultural mandate and our understanding that all of life is sacred, Reformed Christians are more prone to the danger of perverting liberty. Many conclude that we're free to indulge.

Consequently, while engaging and redeeming culture, we often fail to watch our backs, not reckoning with the spell that the world's culture can have on us. Intellectual arrogance completes the cycle by making us certain that it won't happen to us. Armed more with ethical invincibility, alas, than with caution at our total depravity, we go questing for the world's spiritual longings in pop culture's music, movies, and fashion, all too confident that we won't be corrupted in the quest.

Christians from the Reformed tradition who care about evangelism are most in peril. There's a pattern here. When theological and biblical zeal grows limp, we lose sight of how desperately lost we are, and how great and wonderful God's sovereign mercy is. Preoccupied with reforming culture, we grow flabby about embracing the doctrines of grace. After all, Reformed theology is, like, so out of touch with pop culture, and we're busy exercising our liberties by immersing ourselves in that culture.

Meanwhile, the children observing their parents' liberties justified on the grounds of engaging culture usually believe, practice, and worship far less than their parents, a cycle of decline that can expunge all belief in a few short decades. As it did in Puritan New England, lack of vigilance will produce spiritually indifferent, materialistic, and worldly-minded offspring. "Wilderness Zion" soon becomes mere wilderness.

Without self-denial and biblical zeal for precise holiness, without which no generation will see the Lord, Christian liberty simply devolves into license to live a worldly life and presume on grace. "Do not use your freedom to indulge the sinful nature" (Gal. 5:13). First-century Christians were prone to this. So are we.

Pagans on Liberty

Plato wrote: "Excess of liberty, whether in states or in individuals, leads only to excess of slavery." Because he keenly observed human nature, pagan Plato understood this counterintuitive reality: a man who clambers after freedom gets slavery instead.

Likewise, Aristotle in his *Ethics* understood the universal human tendency to overindulge in matters of personal pleasure, and so he urged his readers to strive for the golden mean of virtue. He explained that in matters of self-indulgence, men inevitably err on the side of excess or too much, not on the side of defect or too little.

Take eating, for example. Let's face it: most young men are not tempted to anorexia; you're more inclined to gluttony, food in excess—especially pizza and ice cream! Or how about cars. Most young men's problem is not driving a car too slowly. You're inclined to excess of speed.

In matters where there is no direct command of God, young men must be wise and recognize which side of the golden mean of virtue they must favor. In ice-cream consumption, few young men eat too little; therefore, if a young man wants to act honorably before the Lord with ice cream, he will own up to the fact that his sinful inclination will be excessive eating of ice cream. So he will curb his eating accordingly by eating less than he thinks is appropriate. So with cars and speeding. What he thinks is appropriate is colored too much by his love of self-indulgence.

Freedom and Music

Right up there with cars and ice cream, music ranks high in your love of self-indulgence. But it's not just any music. Secular historians writing about the free-love movement of the 1960s candidly admit that "rock was the music of the rebellious young."

But many protest that it's legalistic to rank an entire genre of music as inappropriate for Christians. "All things are [ours]" (1 Cor. 3:21–23), they quote. And a few still resort to the boggy ground of the "music is neutral" defense.

Prodigious naïveté, however, is required of those who deny the obvious: most rock music, and its derivatives, is carefully designed to make listeners reckless, to give them a throbbing sense of invincibility, an adrenaline-pumping notion of power and freedom, to lower moral restraint, to condition listeners to act on what they feel, and to live outside the boundaries.

The feelings of freedom produced by pop music—let's be clear about this—are not designed to set you free from bondage to sin and to make you a willing bondslave of Christ. Honest young men know that Frank Zappa was dead right with his blunt conclusion: "Rock music is sex."

You know what it does to you, how it makes you feel, what it encourages you to think about. It's why part of you likes it so much. But if you have spiritual wits about you, you know that some music awakens inordinate ideas about freedom—especially sexual freedom.

Therefore, any young man who takes seriously the Bible's command to "avoid sexual immorality" (1 Thess. 4:3) will not allow his ideas about freedom to be shaped by music designed to turn liberty into sexual license. Feed at the trough of pop culture's musical offerings, and—be sure of it—you will distort your liberties. And since freedom is intoxicating, don't expect to know it's happening.

In his music, movies, and other matters that require precise discernment, a wise young man who knows he's called to holiness will err—if erring it be—on the side of restraint and self-denial. A small price to pay for true liberty in Christ.

Double Danger

Dangers from misused liberties have hovered over Christians for centuries. John Calvin refers to the "double danger: mistaken strictness and mistaken laxity." But which is the danger today? Would anyone actually argue that postconservative Christianity is in danger of too much strictness? The golden mean is elusive, but mistaken laxity is the easiest excess to fall into.

Calvin understood that the topic of Christian liberty "is a slippery one and slopes on both sides into error," and so urged in our freedoms that we "plant our feet where we may safely stand," and that we use our liberties "in so far as they help rather than hinder our course."

Regulating the wrongful use of God's gifts, Calvin directs us to use them in accordance with the end for which God gave them. In the exercise of our freedoms, Calvin cautions, "we must resist the lust of the flesh, which, unless it is kept in order, overflows without measure."

Wise young men know how easily we overflow without measure and indulge the sinful nature in our practice of Christian liberty. Whether you are fighting a war for independence from a tyrant, or waging war with the passions that forge fetters in your own soul, be guided by love for your neighbor, and prefer a millstone around your neck rather than cause a little one who believes in Christ to stumble.

Finally, with liberties that you know have turned to license—"Put Watts into 'em, Boys!"

Prayer Resolves

- To regularly remind myself how easily liberty becomes license
- To know the end of liberty: freedom to serve others in Christ's name

Scripture Memory

"You, my brothers, were called to be free. But do not use your freedom to indulge the sinful nature; rather, serve one another in love."

Galatians 5:13

For Discussion

1. In the culture around you, how has American love of liberty decayed into false ideas about freedom?
2. In your own experience, how do you feel the pull to distort freedom into license to do your own thing?

"Paraphrase of Romans 6:1–7"

Too long enthralled to Satan's sway,
We now are slaves no more,
For Christ hath vanquished death and sin,
Our freedom to restore.

Isaac Watts, 1707

For Further Study

Romans 14

4

LEARN SPIRITUAL WARFARE

Psalm 91; Ephesians 6:10–18

When I first heard Ron Boydston tell about his time in Vietnam, I was struck by his well-thought-out grasp of the biblical metaphor of soldiering. He was in the United States Army from 1968 to 1970, and spent a tour of duty fighting in the much-maligned Vietnam conflict, wherein he provided communications for Allied intelligence-gathering efforts. Decode the army-speak, and I'm guessing he was a spy. He graduated from Prairie Bible Institute, and from Seattle Pacific University with a B.A. in religion. After earning an M.A. in print communication at Wheaton Graduate School, Ron has spent his career in magazine publishing. Married with four grown children, Ron is an engaging communicator and a favorite adult Sunday school teacher at his church. Read on.

The War Zone

On a mid-September day in 1969, I stepped off a plane in the Republic of South Vietnam to begin a one-year active-duty assignment with the United States Army.

Out on the runway a fighter jet in camouflage paint, its wings loaded with ordnance, was lifting off on a daytime sortie. Its engine ripped the air with a sense of urgency, underscoring the fact that there was a war going on—and I was now a part of it.

While the plane that I was leaving was bringing fresh American troops to the conflict, I was very aware that other planes were taking other soldiers home from the war, never to fight again in this life; their tours of duty had ended along with their lives. For a soldier entering a war zone, the prospect of death is neither remote nor unexpected; life itself is a currency that is freely spent in the purchase of ideals that rarely come cheap.

The flight had left Oakland, California, many hours ago, and had stopped for fuel at Honolulu, Hawaii, and at a U.S. air base on Okinawa. As we had flown over the South China Sea and slowly descended along the coast of South Vietnam, our eyes were fixed on the small windows that gave glimpses of the country that we had heard so much about in the media and in our Army training.

The temperature was in the 90s, with matching humidity. I was wearing a new set of jungle fatigues and a new pair of combat boots, and the rest of my belongings were packed into a large olive-drab canvas duffel bag. Except for the jet, nothing appeared to be moving very quickly in the heat. I was to find that this was not laziness, but the way to conserve energy in this part of the world.

I was directed to a one-story metal terminal building to wait for a ride to the unit to which I had been assigned. There was no air-conditioning; if anything, it was hotter inside the building than it was outside. Just sitting there, doing nothing, my face started to bead up with sweat.

I had tried to rest during the long flight, but the changes were too momentous, and sleep would not come, so some hours before I had gotten out pen and paper and started the first of many letters that I would produce during the coming months. Now, however, I was too tired even to write. I had traveled halfway around the world, through many time zones, and was farther away from home than I had ever been in my life.

Unencrypted Duty

As I waited, my mind reviewed the events of the previous ten months. I had gone through eight weeks of basic training at Fort Ord, California, and had learned how to march, shoot, and wear a uniform, as well as the definition of "KP," which for me meant 15-hour days toiling over a large sink, cleaning grease-encrusted metal trays on which food for the 125 men in our company had been cooked. This had been followed by another two months of radio school there, where we learned Morse code and how to operate the Army's standard portable radio communications unit, the PRC–25, a backpack-sized radio that accompanied every Army unit in the field.

From there some of us had gone on for further schooling in Fort Gordon, Georgia, where we went through several more months of radio-teletype training, graduating with a basic knowledge of the workings of a 500-watt single-sideband shortwave transmitter-receiver. This radio had a console filled with gauges, switches, and dials, utilized a long-wire antenna, and was paired with a field teletype machine that produced a paper tape, which was then turned into a printed report in a field communications center. The Army used these units, which were designed to be carried as camper-like rigs on the back of pickup trucks, to send encrypted messages from one location to another.

After school some more time passed while we waited for orders. Then, as so many other soldiers had done throughout history, we made a last visit home, put our affairs in order, said our final goodbyes, and then were gone.

Oakland, California, was home to one of the major staging areas for U.S. Army troops heading to Vietnam. Soldiers on their way over were billeted for a few days; here they turned in their stateside issue and were provided with clothing designed for use in a tropical environment.

The Army must have known of my abilities in the kitchen, for no sooner had I gotten there than I was assigned to another round of kitchen police, without even changing out of my dress uniform. Taking off my coat and sticking the end of my tie inside my shirt, I worked for more than eight hours in another kitchen, serving my country by serving meals to my fellow soldiers. What a fitting send-off, I thought, to spend my final hours in the United States toiling away at menial labor. Helping out in the kitchen was not the most glamorous job in the world, but somebody had to do it, and Uncle Sam had picked me especially for the occasion. But somehow it did not seem a very great honor.

War and Faith

In addition to being a soldier, I was also a Christian. The year before I had graduated from Bible college, with a headful of doctrine and Bible knowledge, and the summer before entering the Army had been a counselor at a Christian camp. I believed in a God who was active in the affairs of men and in human history, and who governed the courses of empires and civilizations to accomplish his sovereign will. Was war a part of this grand plan? The answer was of more than theoretical interest to me.

A night or two before shipping out I was sitting on my bunk, one small mattress in a large sea of beds, leafing through a New Testament with Psalms that had been given to me while processing, and came across a section entitled "Scriptures in Time of War." Psalm 91 was listed, so I turned to it and started reading. I had read these words before, while in Bible college, and they were good words; but now that I was headed to a war zone, they assumed a much more applicable meaning.

The psalmist was also acquainted with war and its dangers, but his trust was in the Lord of heaven and earth, and he knew that staying in the presence of the Most High was, irrespective of the circumstances, the safest of places to be. I did not know what the future would bring, but I was going into it with a promise that is the provision of every believer in every age, in circumstances of all types.

Memories, impressions, and thoughts wandered in and out of my mind as I sat in the heat on a hard bench in a military air terminal on my first day in Vietnam. But even with the promises of Scripture still recent in my memory, I did not feel particularly spiritual or even soldierly at that moment. I could feel the sweat not only on my face, but also in my armpits, as it built up and then ran down my sides. It was going to be a long year.

The Longest Year

And that year *was* a long one—one of the longest of my life. Time slowed to a crawl. Long hours became long days, long days became extended weeks, and weeks became interminable months, small eternities unto themselves. It seemed that the Army had, by issuing orders or by some secret battlefield research, tinkered with the space-time continuum in such a way that I would never be able to go home again. My father had been in World War II and had spent three and a half years overseas—had he experienced the same feeling? Had soldiers in other wars? If there was such a thing as a slow boat to nowhere, I was now on it.

But with all that time available to me, I was able to observe the events going on around me and to begin to think about war from a soldier's point of view—not only the conflict that I was in but also the spiritual conflict that the Scriptures speak of. It was one thing to read about warfare while living in the peaceful security of a country thousands of miles away; it was quite another to be in the middle of a war zone, to contemplate what the Bible said, and to try to make some sense of it.

Since that year, I have drawn several conclusions about spiritual warfare, and what physical warfare can teach us about it:

Spiritual Warfare Is Just as Real, and Just as Dangerous, as Physical Warfare

Some Christians think that spiritual warfare is an impersonal conflict between conflicting ideologies that is mostly academic and conceptual, but this is not so. Spiritual warfare is a daily struggle against a very real, very determined, and very capable enemy who is attempting at all costs to prevent the salvation of human souls, and to knock Christians off their spiritual feet. Unlike peacetime soldiers, my comrades and I in Vietnam were not just playing war games, but were pitted against an enemy that wanted to defeat us, and went systematically about trying to achieve that objective. We in turn were trying to return the favor.

Although I was in a relatively secure area, the shooting was never far away, and each night brought the sound of small-arms fire, artillery, and other ordnance. The base on which our compound was situated was regularly hit with rockets, harassing fire mostly, which usually did little damage but which would occasionally hit a barracks or other populated area and kill or injure someone who was sleeping, eating, or otherwise going about their daily routine. It was not a comfortable feeling to live as a human target, but that is just what we soldiers were, and it was never far from our minds, no matter where we were or what we were doing. "Be self-controlled and alert. Your enemy the devil prowls around like a roaring lion looking for someone to devour. Resist him, standing firm in the faith" (1 Peter 5:8–9).

Effectiveness in War Requires Daily and Intensive Discipline

War is hard. There is none of the comfort, ease, and security that characterizes men and nations who are not in a conflict. To be a good soldier requires discipline in thought and discipline in action. There are no musical soundtracks in a war zone. The good guys do not win in two hours while spectators eat popcorn, and the battlefield is not neat and tidy. Good men are hurt or killed, and discipline is mandatory in order to function while facing danger, boredom, and the ambiguities of war, in which clear-cut answers are all too often not evident.

This hardship was most evident for the combat soldiers, but was also a factor for every support soldier as well. Far from home, with little to do in the way of recreation, we had to function in our jobs and find ways to get from one day to the next. Even holidays, which the Army was faithful in observing, were drab and forlorn affairs, civilian celebrations pasted onto an olive-drab background, and if anything served to remind us that life as we had once known it was ten thousand miles away, and accessible only by letters, dreams, and the successful completion of our tours of duty. "Endure hardship with us like a good soldier of Christ Jesus" (2 Tim. 2:3).

Warfare Requires a Willingness to Die

Every soldier, when taking the oath of enlistment, is putting his life on the line, ready to sacrifice himself if need be for the good of his comrades, his unit, and his country. He is entering a high-risk occupation that enormously increases the odds of his being injured or killed.

For fifty-eight thousand United States soldiers, that prospect became a reality, and their names are inscribed on the wall at the Vietnam Veterans Memorial in Washington, D.C. The youngest was fifteen years old, the oldest, sixty-two; seventeen thousand were married; nearly a thousand were killed on their first day in-country, and nearly fifteen hundred were killed on the last day of their scheduled tours. The dead include sixteen chaplains, two of whom were awarded the Medal of Honor. Another 150,000 soldiers spent time in one or more of the field hospitals of Vietnam, but lived to tell the tale. Many were seriously wounded and will carry scars from the war for the rest of their time on this earth.

While most of these deaths came at the hands of the North Vietnamese or the Viet Cong, not all did—some soldiers were killed in vehicle or aircraft crashes, others by friendly fire, and still others in accidents that might have happened anywhere. But they all died in the line of duty, and those of us who survived honor them for giving "their last full measure of devotion."

Likewise, the Christian soldier has put his life on the line, for a much greater cause than any earthly one. Dead to the world and alive unto God, the Christian soldier is free to pursue eternal things. He eats, sleeps, plays, and may marry and raise a family, but always with the knowledge that he has laid down a temporal life in order to lay hold of an eternal one. "They did not love their lives so much as to shrink from death" (Rev. 12:11).

God Is Sovereign—Even in War

Even surrounded by the uncertainty, tedium, and danger of war, God's sovereignty is at work, providing protection for his children. Some see Psalm 91 as promising physical protection in time of war for those who trust in the Lord. While this has sometimes been literally true, many other Christians throughout history have died in battle, and the names of some of them are carved into the black-granite panels of the Vietnam Memorial. Included among those names is that of a friend of mine from Bible college, Norm Bettis, from Osceola, Iowa, who was killed in action in 1969 at the age of 21.

God does not promise us an easy and trouble-free life. But he does promise us his presence no matter what our circumstances. The author of Psalm 91 was well acquainted with war and its dangers, but his foundational trust was not in weapons or armor or military strategy, as important as those items are. It was in the God who walks with his children through all of life, in the physically dangerous places as well as the safe ones. He is the God who walks with us through the valley of the shadow of death, and he knows the way well, for in Christ he has already walked that road, and his presence guarantees that we will never have to walk that road by ourselves. "He who dwells in the shelter of the Most High will rest in the shadow of the Almighty. I will say of the LORD, 'He is my refuge and my fortress, my God, in whom I trust'" (Ps. 91:1–2).

At the end of my year, I came back from Vietnam. Two of the sweetest memories at the end of that endless year were when the wheels of our jet lifted off the soil of South Vietnam, and again when they touched down on U.S. soil; on both occasions the plane erupted with loud cheering from troops who had survived and were now on their way home. Although it has now been many years since I last wore an Army uniform (it is said that you can take a soldier out of the war, but that you cannot take the war out of the soldier), the memories of my time there are never far away; they cause me to be continually grateful, and they point always to the spiritual conflict in which all Christians, whether they are aware of it or not, are engaged.

May God help us to be good soldiers of Jesus Christ.

Prayer Resolves

- To look at the Christian life as a real conflict, and not as entertainment or war games
- To be disciplined in thought and behavior, as befits an effective soldier
- To arm myself with the weapons of righteousness, and to know how to use them

Scripture Memory

"Therefore put on the full armor of God, so that when the day of evil comes, you may be able to stand your ground, and after you have done everything, to stand."

Ephesians 6:13

For Discussion

1. What would you say to Christians who think it is wrong for believers to be a part of the military?
2. What books have you read or movies have you seen about Vietnam? What perspectives do they offer on the war?
3. Paul speaks of "the weapons of our warfare" in 2 Corinthians 10:4. What are those weapons, and how does a young man master their use?

"Triumphant Jesus Bore the Cross"

Yet does the fiend still prowl and lurk,
His schemes upon my heart to work.
But God before me who can stand
When Christ in battle guides my hand?

Douglas Bond, 2007

For Further Study

Joshua 5:13–15; 2 Corinthians 6:4–10; Revelation 19:11–16

5

LEARN TO LEAD

Titus 1:5–9; 2:2, 6–8

Leading by Example

"First he did, and then he taught," wrote Geoffrey Chaucer of the country parson in his celebrated *Canterbury Tales*. After parading a comedy of clerical buffoons and medieval worldlings before his readers, Chaucer changes tacks, drops the satire, and introduces a man of "true consecration."

I'm convinced that he developed this country parson from the example of his contemporary, the saintly John Wycliffe, Morning Star of the Reformation. Unlike the money-grubbing, immoral monks and friars tramping about fourteenth-century England, Wycliffe and his Lollard followers lived by the "Law of Christ." First they obeyed the Bible and then they translated and taught it to the peasant masses throughout the land.

Likewise, doing before teaching must be the defining characteristic of a father's relationship with his son. That is what Paul has in
mind in his letter to Titus and the other Christians on the Isle of Crete.
Fathers—indeed, all Christian men—are on their mettle to be examples, to show young men how to live as God-pleasers. "In everything
set [young men] an example by doing what is good" (Titus 2:7a).

Paul lays the principal responsibility on mature men to "encourage the young men to be self-controlled" (2:6). And there's no better
way to encourage than by example. Thus, fathers must be living out
the virtues Paul tells Titus to be teaching the older men in Crete: "to
be temperate, worthy of respect, self-controlled, and sound in faith, in
love and in endurance" (2:2). It's not enough merely to tell young men
to do good. Fathers and mature men must first do it themselves, living
lives that exemplify these godly virtues, this goodness.

Moreover, just as fathers must live mindful of the eye of God on
our deeds, words, and hidden thoughts, so we must live mindful of the
eye of our sons. They're watching us, and Paul says we must be showing them "integrity, seriousness and soundness of speech that cannot
be condemned" (2:7–8).

Honor Fathers

What is the result of showing these virtues to our sons? The result
is precisely what every man wants.

Men don't always get along. We don't always see eye to eye on
trivial things such as baseball teams or why moose-tracks ice cream is
better than vanilla bean, nor do we always agree on important things
such as theology, worship, and discipline. The result of showing "integrity, seriousness and soundness of speech" to our sons, however, is that
"those who oppose you [will] be ashamed because they have nothing
bad to say about [you]" (2:7–8). Every man who has ever disagreed
with another man wants this.

Nothing undermines the integrity and authority of a man more
than a son who is rebellious, who is disrespectful, and who struts and

swaggers. There will always be those who oppose you—try the world, the flesh, and the devil. But a foolish son must bear to his grave the tragic knowledge that his disrespect and disobedience made his father an object of scorn to the world. Do this to your father, and it will bring him—and you—unmitigated grief.

The inspired poet father in Proverbs put it this way: "Be wise, my son, and bring joy to my heart; then I can answer anyone who treats me with contempt" (27:11). Nothing else weighs in like this. A serious-minded son, standing tall next to his father, walking with integrity, speaking with sound wisdom, brings joy to the heart of his father. But the father whose son is a fool must hang his head in shame and wear the contempt of those who oppose him. Instead of the critic being shamed, the father with a fool for a son is shamed.

I know men whose sons have so shamed them by sinful behavior that those men have forfeited the respect of their adult Christian peers. Still worse, the world waits to pounce on church leaders and fathers whose sons shame them and dishonor them by their folly. What a wonderful thing it is when carping detractors of Christ and his church "have nothing bad to say about us." Perhaps nothing else strengthens the influence of Christian manhood on the culture more than when sons honor fathers and bring joy to their hearts.

Wanted: Church Leaders

But sons might wonder whether this instruction is coming a bit early. Sons are "youngers," not "elders," after all, and Paul's context is helping Titus find the right men to lead in the church on Crete. A tough job, especially among Cretans known as perpetual "liars, evil brutes, lazy gluttons" (Titus 1:12).

An essential characteristic of men worthy of being overseers of the church is that their "children believe and are not open to the charge of being wild and disobedient" (1:6). In other words, men are qualified to lead in Christ's church who have been good fathers, who have been showing their sons the virtues required by men who can stand

59

tall before the slings and arrows of the world, who will not be held in contempt, who will put their critics to shame because of the way their children—their sons—live self-controlled and obedient lives.

Young men involuntarily grow older, but they don't involuntarily grow wiser. Few things are as unbecoming in a man as chronological age without maturity. "How ill white hair becomes a fool and jester," Shakespeare put it. You will never become a skillful leader by setting your sights on play. You must set goals now, cultivate manly appetites and habits now, and make it your chief business to grow up now— or you will never be fit to lead in your home, your work, or Christ's church.

Self-control and Discipline

What are the virtues that capable leaders must master? Paul tells you. Learn to love what is good, and learn to be self-controlled. Hence, an elder's children can't be "open to the charge of being wild." Being wild is the opposite of being self-controlled. Wild things are outside of the boundaries; they live without definitions, without fences, without submission, without restraint. Wild things are not fit to lead.

Therefore, leaders must be self-controlled because they are in charge—that is, they are, to various degrees, in control of men and situations. Since leadership so easily degenerates into bullying tyranny, young men must master self-control before they are fit to control others.

In the high calling of church leadership, men must be "self-controlled, upright, holy and disciplined" (1:8b). That is, ruling elders must prove themselves to be men who live within the boundaries, who play by the rules, who keep the code, who uphold the law. Ruling elders must be like Paul's athlete in 1 Corinthians 9:25 who has entered into "strict training."

You will be a leader someday. Your generation will be the future leaders of the church, the teaching elders, the ruling elders, and the deacons. What kind of leader will you be? Will you be wild—and lead men to hell? Or will you be disciplined and self-controlled—and lead men to heaven?

I Confess

Though it may seem counterintuitive, a nonnegotiable of exercising authority is that you be under authority. Our Puritan forebears summed up the work of the church as preaching, sacrament, and discipline. An elder in the church, a man who is charged with the holy responsibility of ruling, must be guided by the discipline of the confessional standards of the church.

Many Christians are quick to object, "No creed but Christ; no law but love." In many circles it is a mark of faithfulness that you no longer subscribe to the creedal Christianity of the Reformation and the early church. We have the Bible, after all. What more do we need? The argument sounds so convincing. But invariably the people who have stopped reading the great Reformed confessions are the people who vilify them as extrabiblical, man-made, and even heretical.

Yet few Christians would dare suggest that because the Bible speaks so much about civil government, there is no need for constitutional law. Would anyone but a rank anarchist say, "No civil law but love, no civil creed but be nice to people"? Such nonsense spells civil chaos. So in the church, breezy scorn for the biblical creeds of the church spells spiritual chaos.

A new Christian I was conversing with, thrilled with new discoveries on every page of his Bible, was also reading the Westminster Confession of Faith. He made a perceptive observation. "If the church just followed these confessions," he said, "we wouldn't have so much error and confusion."

Ironically, revising or reinterpreting confessional standards is precisely how mainline unbelief has taken such intractable hold of so many American churches. If you want to truly know Christ and proclaim him to the world, the solution is not to remove the systematic doctrinal foundations of the creeds. That's what the liberal churches have done. The best confessional standards, far from directing Christians away from Christ, are actually the most enduring defense of what the Bible teaches about Christ.

Read your Bible first and last. But also read the confessions and see if the best of them do not clearly and biblically define the deity of Christ and his substitutionary atonement for sinners. Master the best of the confessions on Christ or on any other doctrine, and you're equipped to see the wolf of false doctrine before it slinks into the fold and devours the sheep, now and in the generations to come.

The same men who taught *sola Scriptura*, "the Bible alone," diligently studied the Scriptures to see what they "principally taught," then carefully, collaboratively wrote confessions of faith. Christ, in fact, was the creed of Samuel Rutherford, Thomas Goodwin, and the other faithful, gifted men who made up the Westminster Assembly, and thus, the confession and catechisms they crafted are scrupulously faithful to the "Law of Christ."

I Sort of Confess

Why do we need standards? Confessions provide order and boundaries in every age, and are all the more critical in our day, when revisionism guides academic and political discourse. Confessional Christianity keeps each generation from arrogantly reinventing the theological wheel and so driving the church off the cliff of error. No doubt, unthinking, unfeeling adherence to creeds has killed its thousands, but antidoctrinal, undisciplined, how-it-makes-me-feel religion has killed its tens of thousands. Clearly, the latter is the real danger in an age such as ours that scorns discipline and rules.

Paul says that real men who lead must be disciplined. A confession is a disciplined summary of the Bible's teaching that has stood the test of time and that is agreed on by men who minister within the precincts of a denomination. Just as a young man must be disciplined in his adherence to a civil constitution in his country, so a young man must learn to subscribe and adhere to sound doctrine laid out in a theological confession.

The Westminster Confession gives me theological self-control. It reins in my wildness. It exposes my arrogance when I entertain the notion that I'm more enlightened than those ancient roughs writing in the 1640s. Every time I actually open the confession on the doctrine in question, I'm profoundly humbled by the searching clarity, the breadth of biblical wisdom, and the timeless relevance of the confession. It corrects me, and disciplines me, and makes me put my hand on my mouth.

Prepare to lead, and you will be equipped to withstand the allure of revisionist ideas creeping into even the best of denominations today. Believe it, during your future watch on the decks of church orthodoxy, there will be new assaults on confessional standards. Young man, be ready, and stand where the ancients have stood.

Danger within the Gates

B. B. Warfield, the great Princeton theologian, whose high view of the Bible made him a tireless defender of the Westminster Confession, of creedal subscription, and of the doctrinal standards of Reformed Christianity, wrote, "The chief danger to Christianity . . . is corrupt forms of Christianity itself which menace from time to time the life of Christianity."

The church is "endangered more by subversion from within," writes Albert Mohler, "than from outside attacks." However biblical and faithful its proponents insist their revisionist agenda is, revision is always reduction. Christian young men who will lead in the next generation must beware of the danger within the gates.

New challenges will have arisen by the time you're in leadership, but revision advocates looming menacingly on my horizon want to redefine biblical terms such as *justification*, *imputation*, and *election*. Professor of historic and systematic theology R. Scott Clark shows just how far outside the standards some revisionists want to move: "According to them, every baptized person is elect and united to Christ through baptism, but election and union can be forfeited through faithlessness." You will read nothing like this in the Westminster Confession of Faith—or in your Bible.

Still other revisionists discredit what the great confessions have taught about church discipline and suspension from the Lord's Table. Though revisionists always say they're being more faithful than the confession, revision always conforms orthodoxy to present-day agendas and reduces the great confessions to the priorities of a moment.

When Matthew Parker, Queen Elizabeth I's compromising archbishop, revised the work of Thomas Cranmer and the 42 Articles, what remained was a pale shadow of the once-great Reformed confession of the Church of England. In the next generation it was William Laud who made Parker look orthodox. "Laud's Liturgy" created such disorder that Puritans by the thousands fled the country—to America.

Just as the Apostles' Creed or the Nicene Creed would cease to be what they are if they were revised, so would the Westminster Confession, the Heidelberg Confession, or the Philadelphia Confession. Taking the knife to the confessional standards is an impertinence against the integrity of our Christian heritage.

If the revisionists were honest about their concerns for biblical orthodoxy, they ought simply to write a new confession and seek subscribers to it. They don't do this, of course, because it would mean too clean a break with their vows, too clear a declaration of their exceptions with the standards.

Therein lies another important function of the standards. They expose those who no longer adhere. If someone's list of exceptions has grown so great that he feels strongly about revising the standards to fit with his pages of exceptions, the standards have a provision for this, too. It's time to keep one's vows and present all exceptions to the brothers. It's their job to determine whether someone's exceptions "strike at the vitals of religion."

Liturgical Fidgit

In C. S. Lewis's day, revisionists were once again sharpening their knife on the Anglican confessional and liturgical standards. This frustrated Lewis. "It looks as if they believed people can be lured to go to church by incessant abridgments [and] simplifications of the service." Lewis prophetically understood that revision always degrades worship: "Novelty, simply as such, can have only an entertainment value."

Lewis knew that thoughtful Christians don't go to church to be entertained. Worship ought so to direct our minds to God that the minister, the building, the stained glass, the other worshipers, the liturgy itself disappear and only God remains. "Every novelty prevents this. It fixes our attention on the service itself, and thinking about worship is a different thing from worshipping." Lewis urged caution on revision because "it is easy to break eggs without making omelets. The good to be done by revision needs to be very great and very certain before we throw that away." All the uncertainty and newness of revision "lays one's devotion waste."

Lewis wished revision-minded pastors remembered that the Lord charged Peter to "feed my sheep," not "try experiments on my rats, or even, teach my performing dogs new tricks." He concluded with a call for "permanence and uniformity" in liturgy. He called the love of novelty and revision the "liturgical fidgit" of the church. Finally, if revision is needed, he believed it should be "here a little and there a little; one obsolete word replaced in a century."

Hold Fast

As a young man prepares for the high calling of church leadership, he must learn now to be "self-controlled, upright, holy, and disciplined" (Titus 1:8b). Learn now to be a man who lives within the boundaries, who plays by the rules, who keeps the code, who holds fast to truth. Learn, as Paul tells you, to love what is good and to be self-controlled.

Do not be "open to the charge of being wild." Remember, wild things are outside of the boundaries; they live without definitions, without fences, without submission, without restraint. Because wild things refuse to follow, they are unfit to lead.

A real man, a leader in the church, must be sound in doctrine. He is not at liberty to be wild. Therefore, young men must train to be leaders who will be self-controlled, to exercise authority while submitting humbly to authority. This disciplined self-control is learned by the example of your father and godly men in your life.

Go into "strict training." Master the "Law of Christ." In your leadership, cheerfully subscribe to doctrinal, confessional truth and never be shaken. "Stand where the ancients have stood. Wise once, wise evermore."

Prayer Resolves

- To set my mind on leadership
- To cultivate the essential virtues of godly leadership now

Scripture Memory

"Encourage the young men to be self-controlled. In everything set them an example by doing what is good."

Titus 2:6–7a

For Discussion

1. Discuss other areas in which "No creed but Christ; no law but love" doesn't work.
2. What are the strengths and dangers in confessional Christianity?
3. What are the strengths and dangers in nonconfessional Christianity?

"The Church's One Foundation"

Though with a scornful wonder
We see her sore oppressed,
By schisms rent asunder,
By heresies distressed,
Yet saints their watch are keeping;
Their cry goes up, "How long?"
And soon the night of weeping
Shall be the morn of song.

Samuel Stone, 1866

For Further Study

Proverbs 15:10; compare: Westminster Confession of Faith,
Heidelberg Confession, London Confession

6

LEARN TO BE
A DANIEL

Daniel 1

Bob Case, founder and director of World Journalism Institute, is one of the most versatile individuals I know. He owned his own business, was a university professor of philosophy and great books, was intimately involved in politics in the Reagan years, was a member of Phi Kappa, the Society of Christian Philosophers, and the National Association of Scholars, was the founding chairman of the Francis Schaeffer Institute, and was a member of the board of directors of God's World Publications and WORLD *magazine. Currently he directs World Journalism Institute, dividing his time between the New York City headquarters at The King's College in the Empire State Building and the new West Coast office in Tacoma, Washington. From his wide-ranging knowledge and experience, Dr. Case has written an important letter to young men. Read the mail!*

Dear Son,

I am writing this letter to you to put into words, lest I forget, the importance of claiming the world of ideas as your own. It is your inheritance as a Christian young man. The foremost example I can think of is Daniel, the young Jewish lad who lived around 600 BC in a culture that was at least indifferent and even hostile to his deepest-held convictions.

Now, we have read of Daniel in the lions' den and Shadrach, Meshach, and Abednego in the fiery furnace. But I want to emphasize what these four young Hebrew lads were doing at the Babylonian court of Nebuchadnezzar in the first place: they were there to study at the royal academy of Babylon.

They were, in effect, young college students, probably teenagers like you, Son.

The experience of Daniel will be remarkably parallel to your experience as a young college student. You will probably find yourself to be an exile in a strange and hostile land, just as Daniel was, because we live in a post-Christian society. And yet Daniel 1 suggests that it is good for you as a Christian to profit from the secular knowledge of the day. Daniel 1 points out the trials, temptations, and pressures that you may face, but it also suggests how you are to deal with these trials, temptations, and pressures. Young Daniel was able to learn the knowledge of the Babylonians without compromising the least doctrinal or moral point. In fact, Daniel, Shadrach, Meshach, and Abednego were able to excel at the University of Babylon, their faith actually enabling them to outperform their pagan counterparts on Babylonian terms. Let me explain my take on this chapter.

Recruiting the Best

The first two verses of the book of Daniel record how the Babylonian king Nebuchadnezzar waged war against Jerusalem, took its leading citizens and the king (Jehoiakim) into captivity in 605 BC, and then desecrated the holy temple, blasphemously offering the holy vessels of the sanctuary to the service of the chief Babylonian god, Marduk (Dan. 1:1–2; 4:8). Nebuchadnezzar was oppressive, ruthless, and cruel. Babylon was at such enmity with God that it became a type and a foreshadowing of the reign of Antichrist in Revelation 18. And yet we read this in Daniel 1:3–4:

> Then [Nebuchadnezzar] ordered Ashpenaz, chief of his court officials, to bring in some of the Israelites from the *royal family* and the *nobility*—young men without any physical defect, handsome, showing *aptitude for every kind of learning, well informed, quick to understand*, and *qualified to serve* in the king's palace. He was to teach them the language and literature of the Babylonians.

Apparently, Nebuchadnezzar chose only people with specific physical and intellectual gifts. Although he wanted "young men" to be "without any physical defect" and "handsome" and from the upper class ("royal family," "nobility"), the rest of his list sums up the intellectual prerequisites for receiving a successful Babylonian education twenty-five hundred years ago.

Note that these Jewish students were to be "young," so that they might be teachable and wooed away from their religious heritage and families to become Babylonians in spirit and in thought. In fact, we will see that their very names were changed to help implement this personal, cultural, and worldview transformation. Nebuchadnezzar found Jewish believers with intellectual and leadership gifts and gave these four Hebrew teenagers full economic support—a full-ride scholarship—and commanded that "they were to be trained for three years, and after that they were to enter the king's service" (1:5).

This was a purposeful recruiting expedition into the Jewish subculture to get their best and brightest. Not unlike the activities of our culture and the challenge facing Christian families today.

What were those characteristics which the hostile culture was looking for?

One Must Be "Showing Aptitude for Every Kind of Learning"

That is, one must have the academic skills and techniques that are necessary for advanced vocational and abstract learning. Becoming educated means mastering processes as well as accumulating facts and theories. Having the right appreciation for redeeming the mind is essential for the Christian life. Embracing skills such as reading, writing, managing, manual dexterity, teaching, and problem-solving involving highly specific mental gymnastics is the first step toward a life of stewardship of the gifts God has given one.

One Must Be "Well Informed"

That is, one must already have a fund of sound knowledge that may be built upon with further studies. Foundational knowledge is a base, a sure footing to which other knowledge can be added. Many modern scholars reject the knowledge of the past, thus consigning themselves to repeat the same intellectual mistakes as others before them have done. They willingly restrict their understanding to their own narrow perspectives, making themselves artificially primitive. A well-informed person knows what has been thought before him and is committed to adding to that fund of knowledge.

One Must Be "Quick to Understand"

That is, one must be mentally agile. This person must be able to quickly assimilate and synthesize material that is presented. Understanding material means that one is able to evaluate a given situation and its attendant problems, come up with workable solutions and be able to execute those solutions. "Quick to understand" means that one is able to connect the dots of life's situations in order to draw recognizable and satisfying pictures of reality (cf. Dan. 5:17).

One Must Be "Qualified to Serve"

That is, one must understand that the ultimate goal of education is always service. There is no such thing as education for education's sake. The king was looking specifically for people with intellectual and social abilities that could fit them for influential roles in the Babylonian government and culture as a whole. Jeremiah 29:4–9 records a similar exhortation from the Lord to the exiles. A proper education is critical for opening up spheres of service for the Christian who wants to fulfill the Great Commission of our Lord.

Your Gifts

Nebuchadnezzar was not looking for pointy-headed academics, but men who could lead and shape the Babylonian culture. This Daniel passage shows the value of being qualified to serve from a position of influence.

Son, we see Daniel and the boys put in a position to influence Nebuchadnezzar only because they showed "wisdom and understanding [in every matter] about which the king questioned them" (Dan. 1:20).

These young men had studied and learned Babylonian science (astrology, etc.), technology, mathematics, geometry, philosophy, and literature. And because of this, they were prepared to serve when the occasion presented itself. It is too late to prepare when the call comes.

Son, you, too, need to be ready to answer the call.

These qualities of skill, knowledge, understanding, and service, then, are not universal or natural, but some Israelites had these gifts—just as today some Christians have these qualities. Not every Christian is intellectually gifted for the heavy lifting, but some are (as Paul told the Greek believers at Corinth).

Son, you will come to understand your gifts and talents more in the next few years. While not every Christian is gifted like Daniel, all Christians are called to redeem their minds and bodies by developing their gifts and talents to the fullest extent and then using that redemption to serve others.

It seems clear to me that this three-year Babylonian educational program was the will of God. Daniel, Shadrach, Meshach, and Abednego had received their academic talents from God, after all, and his providence had brought them to this place of learning. Thus, there can be nothing intrinsically wrong with God's children learning "the language and literature of the Babylonians" (v. 4).

Son, I suggest that even though modern American universities and colleges are non-Christian, they would be bastions of Christian fundamentalism compared to the University of Babylon.

Modern Western thought has its origins in a biblical worldview, despite its current departures from and corruption of that grand heritage. Daniel, though, could hardly have read a cuneiform tablet without some reference to pagan deities and mythology. The Babylonians were masters of mathematics, astronomy, engineering, and administration, but their very real discoveries in these fields were thoroughly mythologized in the way they were understood; therefore, their learning was false.

Thus, if Scripture indicates that Babylonian "language and literature" were nevertheless worthy of study, there can be nothing objectionable in a Christian's studying any legitimate field of contemporary thought or trade. For all its problems, it is still probably less infused with error than that of the Babylonians.

Go Pearl-Hunting

Son, the world of ideas is your oyster; go find the pearl.

God's children certainly faced problems, however, in such a Babylonian environment. No sooner had the four Hebrews arrived at court than they encountered a problem that seemed to jeopardize their whole educational opportunity. I find it fascinating that the conflict Scripture records is neither over great worldview issues (such as the merits of the Babylonian creation myth versus the Genesis account of creation, or the existence of the one true God versus the many false gods) nor over important moral issues. Rather, the issue in contention was one that must have seemed to both sides so technical, so minor, and so hard to explain.

The king was honoring these young superstar scholars with a "daily amount of food and wine from the king's table" (v. 5)—lavish, exquisite food for these poverty-stricken student exiles, a generous, even kindhearted gesture on the part of Nebuchadnezzar. Yet that food would not have been in accordance with the Mosaic dietary laws. Not only could the Hebrews not eat certain animals, but even an acceptable animal had to be slaughtered in a certain way. Such rules were absolutely binding on God's people at that time, designed in part to stress God's claim on every single part of life (even cooking and eating), and to ensure that the people of God were measurably different from those people who were not God's possession. How could Daniel explain to the Babylonians this cultural separation, this Hebrew tribal peculiarity? He would seem not only absurdly scrupulous, but—what is worse—arrogant, insulting, ungrateful, and intolerant of local customs.

Son, he wouldn't be politically correct.

It might be similar to our being scrupulous about a biblical view of the Lord's Day concerning work and personal amusements. Nevertheless, Daniel adopted a principle that is absolutely essential for those Christian students trying to follow God in a hostile or indifferent academic environment.

Choose Your Battles

Son, the young Daniel would not compromise God's Word. And please notice that the four young men were scrupulous, but not fundamentalistic.

They knew the liberty they had through faith in the one true God. For instance, they were willing to adopt Babylonian names whose meanings alluded to pagan deities (Dan. 1:7). Wasn't this name-taking a rather liberal compromise on their part? Scripture doesn't seem to think so. These Hebrew youths knew that the false Babylonian gods Bel and Nebo did not exist, so they would not be harmed by a mere name.

In our time, we have midweek church services on *Wednesday*, "the day of Wodan" (a Norse god). And are we enmeshed in a satanic web at church when we worship on *Sunday*, the day set aside for worship of the sun? We can think of other cultural examples of using culturally acceptable but disagreeable language that cannot deter the fundamental issues of right and wrong.

Even so, the dietary laws were different. These practices set God's people apart and gave them identity as people of God. These faithful lads had to ask themselves what would govern their obedience and self-definition: the "king's table" with its luxury and prestige and social acceptance, or the law of Moses with its austere and strange demands in a foreign culture. They had to make a choice—to be assimilated into the dominant pagan culture by conformity to the pagan cultural orthodoxy, or to remain distinctively different, exiles and outcasts, "aliens and strangers" (Heb. 11:13; 1 Peter 2:11) in and to their surrounding society. They resolved not to defile themselves by capitulation to the Babylonian cultural pieties. A young Christian scholar, like Daniel, must be very hesitant to adjust the faith in even the smallest doctrinal or moral principle. Our Babylonian watching world is quick to notice our smallest compromise.

Leaders Win Followers

And yet Daniel was able to resolve the dilemma in a winsome way without compromising his principles.

Son, notice that the four did not tip over the "king's table": they didn't stand up and condemn the Babylonians for eating pork.

Rather, with courtesy and respect, Daniel went to the proper authority to ask permission to keep God's law (Dan. 1:8). And this is what you will be increasingly asked to do in our own Babylonian culture.

As important as it was to avoid unclean food, Daniel understood the biblical principle that he must respect all human authorities, even pagan ones (Rom. 13:1–7), and that to avoid one sin (ritual defilement) by committing another sin (rebellion) is to gain nothing.

Son, biblical submission is a radical spiritual discipline. It embodies self-denial, and bold faith in the sovereignty of God. To see God's authority looming behind all human authority (Dan. 4:34–35; 5:21–28;

6:26) and to see how God employs secular authority for our good is to acknowledge God's providence reigning over every part of life.

So Daniel addressed these pagan administrators with courtesy and humility: he referred to himself and his buddies as "your servants" (1:12). And, as a result of his humility and his openness to pagan authority, the Babylonian leaders positively responded to him. Moreover, Daniel was being aided by the living God (1:9). The most hostile individual can be softened by the action of God.

God Is Sovereign

But, Son, worldly acceptance might not happen in every case. Hebrews 11:32–38 alludes to Daniel's earthly victory, and then gives examples of earthly defeats (but heavenly victories). So we act like Christians, and leave the consequences up to a sovereign God.

And even in Daniel's situation, despite this God-given sympathy for their plight (Dan. 1:9), the chief officer at first turned them down. The officer had an understandable concern: if the four Hebrew students did not seem as healthy as their Babylonian peers, the king would assume that the officer was not taking care of them as well as he should (1:10). Nebuchadnezzar's management style was not to fire ineffective employees but to cut off their heads (Jer. 22:25; Dan. 3:6).

Still, despite this initial setback, Daniel did not give up. He went to the next administrator in the chain of command, the "guard," and he proposed a creative alternative (Dan. 1:12–16).

Daniel's proposal addressed both sides of the stalemate. The Babylonian university authorities were concerned with the boys' health—that point must be preserved. And the Hebrew teenagers were concerned about the dietary laws—that point must be preserved. But were God's people forbidden to eat everything from a Babylonian kitchen? If not, what could they eat? Daniel realized that the meat might not be kosher, but there was no reason why they could not eat the vegetables, which were not covered by the Mosaic code. They could thus still eat from the king's bounty, thereby avoiding giving offense, without violating their Mosaic-instructed consciences. As for the matter of their health, Daniel proposed a test, a sort of controlled experiment, to determine objectively whether or not the officer's fear was well founded.

Whether God was working a special miracle to sustain their health or whether Scripture is simply recognizing that a vitamin-rich diet of vegetables is healthier than ten days of gourmet meat is not the point—Daniel was vindicated, and the university was pleased.

Son, it was a win-win solution. The legitimate political interests of the pagan university were maintained, and the legitimate religious interests of the four believing students were maintained.

Behave Like Daniel

Daniel's behavior is a model for the interaction between the Christian and his non-Christian culture: understand the problem, form an alternative solution, and be willing to test the solution.

Daniel 1:17 states that academic pursuits and accomplishments not only are pleasing to God, but are gifts that he bestows. All knowledge and understanding come under the sovereignty and the gift of God, thereby sanctioning the whole range of human learning—vocational and academic. Such all-inclusiveness gains even more force when one remembers that the Scripture is referring to the knowledge of Babylon, a culture surely more ignorant of God, more immoral and more evil, than is any modern secular culture.

Son, the Jewish lads' knowledge of God's Word gave the four boys an enormous advantage over the Babylonian intellectual establishment (1:18–21). In the final examination, God granted them success. Specifically, God's children, reared in the sophisticated intellectual climate of Babylon, and at the same time saturated with the truth of God's Word, proved themselves "ten times better" than their peers.

Son, what an advantage you should have, being freed from the credulities or beliefs of secular humanism and the stifling limitations of scientific materialism. Modern Christian teen scholars, like Daniel and his colleagues, can strive to meet modern thought on its own terms and to succeed and to exert their influence, even in the modern-day University of Babylon.

Son, I pray that our God may grant you the ability and humility to use your intellectual gifts and training (and therefore advantages) for the service of humankind and the glory of Christ.

Prayer Resolves

- To be a good steward of the intellectual and physical gifts that God has given me
- To be opportunistic in using those gifts in whatever circumstances I find myself
- Always to respect and honor the human authorities placed over me

Scripture Memory

"We demolish arguments and every pretension that sets itself up against the knowledge of God, and we take captive every thought to make it obedient to Christ."

2 Corinthians 10:5

For Discussion

1. Can you exercise your intellectual gifts more faithfully at a Christian college than at a state or private non-Christian college? Explain.
2. Is it more appropriate for a Christian student to major in a social science or in business? Explain.
3. Just because you have intellectual gifts, must you go to college? Why or why not?

"Take My Life, and Let It Be"

Take my life, and let it be consecrated, Lord, to thee.
Take my moments and my days; let them flow in ceaseless praise.
Take my hands, and let them move at the impulse of thy love.
Take my feet, and let them be swift and beautiful for thee.

Frances Havergal, 1874

For Further Study

Genesis 37:36; 39–41; Colossians 1 and 2; *Postmodern Times*, by
Gene Edward Veith

7

LEARN TO WORK

Ephesians 6:5–9; Colossians 3:22–24

Sweat and Money

When my son Desmond was nine, he developed an obsession with buying gifts for his family at Christmas. But there was a problem. He had no money. I helped him make up a sign on which he wrote something like this: "Need money for Christmas gifts. Will work cheap. References available." And then the phone number. Desmond and I stapled the sign to the telephone pole in front of our house. He stationed himself at the window and waited.

During dinner that evening, the phone rang. "This is what's wrong with the world," said an excited voice on the other end of the line. "Kids don't know how to work."

I explained that we wanted ours to learn how to work. He cut me off.

"I'm standing here in front of this sign thinking, 'This is the kind of kid I need,' and I'll pay him what he's worth."

I explained that we wanted him to get paid only if he was actually worth something on the job. The voice grew more excited.

"Listen, I'm rebuilding my house, and I need lots of grunt labor. How old is this kid?"

"Nine," I replied.

"Nine?"

"But he has two older brothers," I added.

"Send all three of them down tomorrow morning at 6:30—sharp."

That was over three years ago. Three of my sons work regularly for our contractor neighbor, who actually cares a great deal about their safety and about getting as much work as he can out of them. The older ones now run power tools, frame walls, haul equipment, set up scaffolding, and perform many other skilled activities. He pays them well, and yes, he has not paid them a few times when he and I decided they hadn't earned it.

In a slouching, hang-loose culture, one of the most important things that a young man must learn is how to work, how to be worth a great deal to an employer, how to take initiative, how to anticipate tasks and do them before being asked. In short, Christian young men ought to be the most valuable asset that any employer has on the job.

Work Like a Buckle-Head

Medieval Roman Catholicism taught that good works were essential to earn one's salvation. These good works took on various forms, but included acts of penitence to pay for the temporal punishment of sins. Rejecting the Roman error, Martin Luther and John Calvin, nevertheless, did believe in work. But work was a result, not a cause, of salvation. Good works were the fruit, not the root, of salvation.

Reformers embraced with gusto the biblical doctrine of calling, whereby it was understood that all of life was sacred, including work. Every task was to be done as an act of service to God. If you were a plowman, or a milkmaid, or a blacksmith—however lowly your task in the world's eyes, you were to do your work before the face of God as an expression of love and service to Christ.

From the Reformed doctrine of calling emerged the Puritan work ethic, the moral and spiritual foundation on which the current American work ethic totters precariously. Puritans saw every activity as sacred and, therefore, as eternally significant. Puritan Richard Baxter urged his flock in Kidderminster, "Promise not long life to yourselves, but live as those that are always uncertain of another day."

"This approach to life," wrote Leland Ryken, "resulted in three vintage Puritan traits: the ideal of the God-centered life, the doctrine of calling or vocation, and the conviction that all of life is God's." If all of life is to be lived to the glory of God, if the chief end of man is to glorify and enjoy God forever, then work, the thing we spend a great portion of our lives doing, is to be both enjoyed and done to the glory of God.

While seventeenth-century detractors of the Puritans dubbed them disciplinarians, today's critics accuse them of being killjoy buckleheads. Some construct a caricature of Puritans moping around, slaving away to redeem themselves from original sin, nobody cracking a smile or having any fun in the process.

These absurd constructs are favorites of postmoderns looking for excuses to vilify Christianity and free-market economics in one fell swoop. "The Puritans," continued Ryken, "aspired to be worldly saints—Christians with earth as their sphere of activity and with heaven as their ultimate hope." This is illustrated by the exhortation that Baxter offered to workers: "Write upon the doors of thy shop and chamber, 'This is the time on which my endless life dependeth.'"

Young men ought to think this way about everything they do, but especially about work. Work is the proving ground of faith. "Faith without deeds is dead," wrote James. A great deal of your own happiness and that of your future wife and children will depend on your having developed a heartfelt Puritan work ethic in your youth. Those who do will be useful to both God and man. Those who don't will be useful to neither.

But a host of impediments stand in the way of a young man's developing a biblical work ethic.

Men, Beware

Someone has said, "I love work; I can sit and watch it for hours." We laugh, but laziness is no joke. It's one of the great impediments that keep young men from learning to work like a man. "Diligent hands will rule," wrote the wise man, "but laziness ends in slave labor" (Prov. 12:24). Make a joke of hard work, and get ready for a life of drudgery and disappointment.

A friend of mine commented after leading teenagers on a missions trip to build a house in Mexico, "Once I helped the boys figure out that standing around wasn't cool, we got lots done." Conforming to teen cool will never put you in the path of diligence and hard work. Cool is a setup for laziness. Laziness is a setup for slavery.

You've all seen the I'd-rather-be-playing license-plate frames. Someone once gave me one. "I'd rather be sailing," it declared. As much as I enjoy sailing, I never put it on the car. Do I want to display that message while driving to church? While taking my wife out to dinner? Or while on my way to work? Live for play, and you will never learn to work like a man.

Another barricade that a hang-loose culture constructs against a biblical work ethic is the lottery. Perhaps one of the most destructive institutions since legalized slavery, state-sponsored gambling enslaves millions of men. They play the lottery, motivated by the desperate hope of getting rich quickly and without working for it, the two death blows to a biblical work ethic. A young man who is serious about working for eternity will not waste an instant of his life playing the lottery.

Work to Play

"Do not work for food that spoils, but for food that endures to eternal life" (John 6:27). Here our Lord gives us the summation of how you and I are to think about work. We are to cultivate a heavenly motivation for all earthly activities, including work. The unbeliever works for basic needs such as food, clothing, and shelter. And for his inalienable right to entertainment and amusement.

It's all part of the American Dream. Work hard for food that spoils, and for entertainments that fade and bring only fleeting satisfaction, leaving a void of pleasure that must be filled by the disposable income from the next paycheck. "Thank God it's Friday." Most men work with their eyes on the weekend. They work so they can play. The workweek is a necessary drudgery to get to the weekend and play.

As men's understanding of work has shifted away from the Puritan work ethic, not surprisingly, so has their view of rest and the Sabbath. The weekend is no more for God than the workweek was. Rest is trumped by play and entertainment, and we believe it's all ours by right.

Work for Eternity

You must find the middle way between working to provide for your family and trusting in God to provide. The middle way is difficult, but the scale tips most easily to working for your own prosperity. "You have far more cause to be afraid of prosperity," wrote Baxter, "than of adversity; of riches, than of poverty."

Hence, a wise young man prepares to maintain the golden mean of tension between the biblical obligation to work and the biblical promise that God provides for all our needs. Trim the sails too hard to duty and work, and you become a driven workaholic who stays late on the job, to the neglect of his wife and children. Let out the mainsheet on trusting in God to provide, and you throw duty to the wind and become lazy, irresponsible, and good for nothing but play.

"Whatever you do, work at it with all your heart, as working for the Lord, not for men, since you know that you will receive an inheritance from the Lord as a reward" (Col. 3:23–24a). The sure way to find the golden mean is to work for an audience of one.

This requires faith. It demands that you have and maintain a clear sight of your heavenly inheritance, the celestial reward that must be your ultimate goal. Work is seen in your world as a temporal activity, something that has nothing to do with faith in an unseen world. But it is not so. And our Puritan forebears understood this better than anyone down through the generations of God's people.

But you must maintain this vigilance and pass it on to your children—or else. Puritan preacher Cotton Mather wrote that "religion begat prosperity, and the daughter consumed the mother." Tragically, within a generation in Puritan New England, coldness descended on the "wilderness Zion," and in places it became just a wilderness. Far from being a "model of Christian charity," colonists gossiped, bickered, and criticized their neighbors. A handful of colonists in Salem village attempted to solve their petty disagreements by hanging some of their neighbors for witchcraft.

Maintaining heavenly-mindedness in work is critical to generational faithfulness. Work merely for wealth—and lead your sons to hell.

Economics and Dirty Hands

Parallel to the American Declaration of Independence from British tyranny, another important event happened in 1776. Scottish economist Adam Smith's book *Wealth of Nations* (Isa. 60:11) was published. Smith argued for *laissez-faire* economics, a marketplace where the government kept its hands off private property and personal wealth so that individuals would have an incentive to work hard and solve problems by producing new products and services that would benefit society.

Smith didn't believe government needed to insert its regulatory hand into the economy because there was already an "invisible hand" guiding the world and, thus, guiding the marketplace.

Vilified by liberal politicians and by market-bashing Hollywood leftists, Smith's free-market capitalism gets blamed for human greed and poverty. Curiously, these same critics wax eloquent when extolling what they consider to be the virtues of Karl Marx's economic theory.

Their solution is to empower government to redistribute wealth so that there will be a classless society. It sounds like such a nice thing to let the government do. Advocates of Marxian economics or communism make it sound so righteous. Liberal politicians create an either/or fallacy whereby, if you are opposed to government redistribution of wealth, you must not care about the poor, and you want the rich to get richer off the backs of the workers.

Governments slap the "invisible hand" in many ways, but the Great Society of the 1930s created one of the most destructive phenomena to a biblical work ethic: the minimum-wage law (MWL).

Nobody is helped in the long run by this attempt at shoving aside the "invisible hand" in the market and allowing government to insert its soiled hands by dictating to employers what they must pay workers. My son Desmond was not worth the legal minimum wage when he started working for our neighbor. But there's only one way to learn: pick up that shovel and start digging. Alas, the soiled hand of the MWL ensures that lots of young men will go through life with soft, pretty hands.

Entry-level workers may never learn how to be worth their wages when their pay is set not by how hard and skillfully they work, but by government edict. Furthermore, those who are worth more will be paid less than they are worth because employers are forced to pay higher minimum wages to the unskilled new employees.

Under the crushing thumbscrew of government regulation, many employers are forced to mechanize, thereby diminishing available job opportunities and increasing unemployment. Some are forced to outsource manufacturing to willing workers in countries without an MWL.

Liberals love attacking these efforts to produce the best product at the best price, and then they scramble to create further regulation that will punish all those evil employers—you know, the ones who invest the money, produce the products, and create all those jobs.

It's logical absurdity, however, to blame capitalism for human greed and exploitation. How can a system that allows the greatest opportunity for any worker who will create goods and services for his neighbors, that invites anyone who wants to contribute, be blamed for exploiting the contributors? Blaming the free market for poverty is like blaming paper and pencils when students fail tests.

The free market is merely leveling the playing field, and because it leaves that field level and accessible to all who want to participate, it is the best system in a fallen world. Blaming capitalism for greed and poverty deflects from the root problem. Human beings are greedy sinners who are prone to love money and steal it from their neighbors. The fault lies with human sin, not capitalism. Those who say otherwise understand little about human motivation—or human depravity.

Transformed Work Ethic

C. T. Studd, the great pioneer missionary, grew up in a home where independent wealth lay all about him. His father bred and raced horses and modeled for his three sons the life of the English gentleman: live for pleasure; use your wealth for play; fritter away your intellect and best years on gratifying diversions. In short, your time and your money are your own. Eat, drink, and be merry. But whatever you do—don't work.

Then, by the power of the Spirit of God, C. T. Studd's father was converted. His entire lifestyle was transformed. He sold his racehorses, and began praying for and urging the gospel on his sons. He reconfigured his country mansions so that he could invite the neighborhood to hear gospel preachers such as D. L. Moody.

God answered his father's prayers, and C. T. Studd was saved. He eventually counted his substantial wealth and status as loss for the sake of Christ. In a letter to his mother he wrote, "Finding out so much about not only the needs of the heathen, but also of the poor in London has increased my horror at the luxurious way I have been living; so many suits of clothes of all sorts, whilst thousands are starving and perishing of cold."

A Cambridge champion at cricket, tennis, and rowing, Studd left athletic glory, riches, and luxury behind and followed Hudson Taylor to China. Guided by his life motto, "If Jesus Christ be God, and died for me, then no sacrifice can be too great for me to make for him," with prodigious energy, Studd later labored to establish Christian missions in India and Africa. By the grace of God, he was a young man who knew how to work, and he knew what to work for: food that endures to eternal life. So must you, if you are to live a life that is useful for the glory of God.

Divine Taskmaster

Just as God can speak through the mouth of a donkey, he calls hardworking young men to be preachers and missionaries; and just as he gives ravens food and can use ravens to bring his children food, so God requires you to work—or not eat.

This principle is an important part of a young man's sanctification. Learn to work and work hard. Be the best employee. Never be late to work. Take initiative. Work with integrity and gratitude to your employer. But do all of this ultimately to be seen of God, not of men.

This will require self-control. The pull to work for all the cool stuff you can buy with your paycheck is as powerful and destructive as a D–9 Caterpillar yanking out a cottonwood tree by the roots. Self-control in this regard will require constant prayer. You will need to write on the door of your workplace, "This is the time on which my endless life depends."

A young man who works for his divine Employer will do his work with excellence. There's no room for shirking when you work for the King of kings. And you will be most productive and profitable when you work to please your divine Taskmaster. When praised for a job well done, you will shift the praise back to your Master. You will tell others that you were able to accomplish such a great task only with God's tools, on his time clock, and with his training and encouragement.

Work—for the night is coming. And learn to work "for food that endures to eternal life" (John 6:27).

Prayer Resolves

- To work for food that endures to eternal life
- To be a diligent worker who works for a divine Employer
- Never to cheat an employer

Scripture Memory

"Whatever you do, work at it with all your heart, as working for the Lord, not for men, since you know that you will receive an inheritance from the Lord as a reward."

Colossians 3:23–24a

For Discussion

1. What problems emerge when I compartmentalize my life into sacred and secular divisions?
2. Discuss the advantage of working as a teenager and being forced to balance other obligations.

"Go, Labor On"

Go, labor on while it is day;
The world's dark night is hast'ning on.
Speed, speed your work,
Cast sloth away . . .

Horatius Bonar, 1843

For Further Study

Proverbs 6:6; 13:4; 20:4; Ephesians 6:5–9

8

LEARN TO SERVE

Mark 16:15

Father, pastor, scholar, and missionary Dr. Dan Steere is an extraordinary individual to call friend. Not only did he teach me how to think and write essays in college (a few years ago), he's still teaching me how to be faithful and how to serve. My most recent lesson came on a teaching mission with him in Uganda. What a joy to see what the Lord is doing in the once-benighted continent of Africa! Dan is field director for Equipping Pastors International (EPI). With boundless energy, he spends his time writing curriculum, training volunteers, preaching in U.S. churches, and traveling to the four corners of the globe, equipping native pastors and teachers in the church throughout many places in the developing world. His is an exciting life, a hectic one—sometimes a dangerous one. But ultimately his is an eternally satisfying life of service to Christ and his worldwide kingdom.

Excitement and Fear

It sounded like fireworks, or maybe a car backfiring. Then people all around me in the crowded streets of Kampala started screaming.

They knew what it was: gunfire. Soldiers were firing their weapons into the crowd—a now-frenzied crowd, scattering in my direction!

Being a missionary in Africa is exciting, but at that moment, fear overtook my excitement. This mixture of excitement and fear often accompanies missionary work. It is exciting to stand before hundreds of spiritually hungry people and share the truth of God's Word, but there are also frightening times, such as when you're completely lost in the bush or facing the business end of an automatic weapon in the city.

The history of Christian missions follows this same pattern. There are periods when the church seems alive with excitement and the gospel spreads like wildfire. And there are other times when the church seems to be afraid—or, worse, content. But we should be excited because we serve a great God who is powerfully building Christ's church around the world. And young men have an important role to play in this drama, for in one sense, Christ has called *all* his people to be missionaries.

A Sobering Lesson

The story of missions begins at Pentecost. Two things happened at that time that set the church on the road to manifesting the worldwide character of Christ's kingdom. First, the Holy Spirit came upon God's people in a powerful way, enabling them to declare the gospel with inexplicable boldness, using languages they'd never learned. Second, when their powerful witness met that cosmopolitan audience, God created over three thousand missionaries in one day. These new missionaries hurried to their homes around the Roman world with the good news of the gospel.

It was a great beginning. But the Jewish church soon forgot the worldwide character of the Great Commission, focusing on evangelizing only Jews. Providentially, the Lord cured this inwardness through the death of Stephen. The resulting persecution drove the believers out of comfortable Jerusalem and into the world. Everywhere they went, they "gossiped" the gospel, telling the people they met about Jesus Christ and his atoning death. In cities such as Damascus and Antioch, hundreds of Gentiles trusted in Christ. The church became increasingly Gentile, confirming that the gospel was for the nations.

There is a lesson here: the Jewish church was born in great excitement through the power of the Holy Spirit. Persecuted, they became missionaries and broadcast the gospel to many nations. Once they had passed the torch, however, they lost their missionary fervor. Rather than remaining ablaze with the light of the truth, they turned inward once more, and eventually their light was snuffed out. The church that loses its passion for missions quickly loses God's blessing and will be superseded by others.

Missions lies close to God's heart, and a healthy church burns to impact the world with the gospel. This fire is stoked by men, young and not so young, who know God's heart and share his passion to show his glory among the nations. This is the engine that drives the church forward.

To the Gentiles

Even during this early persecution, the Lord of the church had his eye on the chief persecutor. Christ intended to make Saul of Tarsus into one of his greatest witnesses. In time, Saul became the apostle Paul: converted on the Damascus road, trained by Christ himself, and uniquely qualified to be the first great missionary of the church. We know a lot about Paul's missionary work because it was divinely chronicled in the book of Acts and in his letters to the churches. But Paul was not the only apostle to carry the gospel to the Gentiles.

While Scripture does not speak of their missions work, history preserves some information on the other apostles. It tells us that Peter eventually ended up in Rome, where he was crucified. John's name is connected with Asia Minor before he was exiled on the island of Patmos in the Aegean. Thomas is said to have taken the gospel to India; Bartholomew preached in Arabia. Of the missionary work of the remaining apostles, we know little more than that they were faithful to God's call—and that all died as martyrs for the faith.

But by far, the most remarkable part of the initial expansion of the church is not the missionary work of the apostles, but that of obedient (and usually anonymous) believers. They were the ones, whether Jews or Gentiles, who took the gospel east into Persia and south to Egypt and Ethiopia. Anonymous missionaries also established churches in Gaul (later France), North Africa, and Spain to the west, while their compatriots preached the gospel in Armenia to the north. These missionaries were so faithful in spreading the gospel that, very early in the second century after Christ, we find Christian churches thriving throughout much of the known world—from Britain to Syria and beyond.

The indomitable spirit of these early Christians is exemplified by Polycarp, the bishop of Smyrna in Asia Minor. He had been a student of the apostle John, and had faithfully preached the gospel for many years. When condemned to death as an old man, he was urged to forsake Christ and save his life. Polycarp replied, "For eighty-six years I have been his servant, and he has never done me wrong: how can I blaspheme my King who saved me?" The enraged crowd burned him alive, but not before he had prayed for them.

In the following centuries, Christianity came to be an integral part of the Roman Empire—to the point that in the early fourth century, the Emperor Constantine declared himself to be a Christian. But at this moment of great triumph, the church turned from missionary activity and began to look inward. Although these were the years when the great creeds of Nicea and Chalcedon were written, the church neglected Christ's commission to take the gospel to the nations. It needed a wake-up call, and God was preparing a loud one.

Gospel Advance; Gospel Retreat

The followers of the false prophet Muhammad poured out of Arabia in the 630s, quickly filling the political and religious vacuum left by a fallen Roman Empire and a complacent church. In less than fifty years, a huge section of formerly Christian territory and an unknown number of believers had been swallowed up by Islam. And the church slept. By the end of that century, all of North Africa was under the Muslim heel—and the church slept.

The Muslims continued on across the Straits of Gibraltar and into Spain, which was largely conquered by 715. They then turned their sights on France and crossed the Pyrenees, only stopping when defeated in the very heart of France by Charles Martel at the Battle of Tours in 732. And except for those areas directly affected by the Muslim invasion, the church largely remained asleep. But on the farthest edge of Europe, the light of the gospel was preserved.

Around the year 400, a young British boy was captured by Irish raiders and sold into slavery in Ireland. In those days, Ireland was a pagan land almost totally ignorant of the gospel. This boy herded swine for six years, and while he worked among the pigs, God worked in his heart. He later wrote, "The Lord opened the understanding of my unbelief, that, late as it was, I might remember my faults and turn to the Lord my God with all my heart; and He had regard to my low estate, and pitied my youth and ignorance, and kept guard over me even before I knew Him . . ." After his conversion, Patrick gave himself to prayer, and when the opportunity came for him to escape, God provided a boat that took him to freedom.

But Patrick was unable to forget Ireland. After returning home, he dreamed one night that the Irish were pleading with him to return: "Please, holy boy, come and walk among us again." Believing this was God's call, he gave himself to theological study and returned to Ireland in 432 to begin his life's work. Despite strong opposition from the pagan Druids and at least twelve attempts on his life, Patrick traveled the length and breadth of Ireland, preaching the gospel. In the course of his thirty-year ministry, he planted nearly two hundred churches and baptized about a hundred thousand converts. Because of his faithfulness, Ireland became a spiritual lighthouse to a darkened Europe.

The historian of missions, Stephen Neill, writes, "Roman culture, which had been almost wholly driven out from the ancient Latin lands, was to know a late and unexpected flowering in the furthest of the Western Isles, and from there to flow back to the continent of Europe."

Following the pattern set by Patrick and a later Irish monk, Columba, the Celtic church sent missionaries into the "wilds" of continental Europe, and as they shared the gospel, they also established schools, monasteries, and churches. Europe remained Christian, the threat of Islam was defused, and the church remained alive in expectation of God's reviving hand.

By the 1200s the Roman Catholic Church had gained such strength that it dominated virtually every aspect of European culture. Yet as the church sank ever more deeply into theological error and chronic corruption, its influence was often more negative than positive. The church needed to be cleansed and revived before true missionary activity could commence again.

A New Dawn

God ignited a revival of the church in 1517 through the preaching and writing of an obscure German monk named Martin Luther. Luther was a biblical scholar who discovered the gospel through Bible study. His uncompromising teaching on justification by faith alone electrified the church and precipitated one of the largest awakenings the church has ever known. What has been called the Protestant Reformation was actually a revival that swept through the deadwood of Roman Catholicism like a brush fire.

As a consequence of the Reformation, the excitement of missions was reborn, and missionaries began to go out from Protestant churches into regions dominated by Roman Catholic errors. The truth of salvation through faith in Christ's works alone spread throughout much of Europe as missionaries preached the gospel openly—sometimes at the cost of their lives. As a result, whole nations aligned themselves with the truth of the gospel.

Besides Martin Luther, the man who did more than any other to spread the gospel in Europe was a Frenchman named Jean Cauvin. John Calvin, as we know him, was an upright and promising young man who had determined to be a scholar. God, however, had other plans. God "subdued his stubborn will" and called him as a missionary to the city of Geneva in Switzerland. Although the pagan Genevans opposed his preaching, and Calvin himself was reluctant at first, he persisted. And Geneva became a haven for persecuted Protestants as well as a pattern for Reformed communities all over the world.

During the years of his ministry, Calvin continually expanded his magnum opus, a handbook of theology for Christians called *The Institutes of the Christian Religion*. He also established a college for training missionaries, many of whom were smuggled into France to spread the truths of the gospel and establish Reformed churches. Calvin's passion for the gospel and love for God's Word inspired thousands. This reluctant missionary became a spiritual father to the following generations of the church.

One of Calvin's true "children," born some two hundred years later, was David Brainerd—a young man to whom God gave a passion for reaching Native Americans with the gospel. Enduring great hardship and struggling with discouragement, Brainerd burned himself out preaching Christ to the tribes along the American frontier. He preached for only five years and died of tuberculosis at the age of twenty-nine. But God blessed his efforts, and after much discouragement, he saw many of his hearers become believers. Brainerd's was a small effort and would have passed unnoticed by history but for his journal. That journal, with its statements of confidence in God's sovereign grace and personal examples of sacrificial love for the lost, was used by the Lord to inspire the modern missionary movement.

God often uses young men as his messengers. Wise young men pour their energy and confidence into doing great things for Christ's kingdom. Oh, may God's grace help you to flee youthful lusts and, like David Brainerd, use your youthful passion for the spreading of the gospel! Reading Brainard's journal will help you to do this.

An English shoemaker named William Carey read Brainerd's journal, and it helped convince him that God was calling him to the mission field. The leaders of his church thought God would convert the heathen without men's help. But Carey disagreed and challenged his fellow pastors with the statement (based on Isaiah 54:2–3), "Expect great things from God; attempt great things for God." He helped to found the Baptist Missionary Society and then in 1793 sailed for India. In evangelism, church-planting, and Bible translation, William Carey set a pattern for the missionaries who followed him. Now called "the father of modern missions," Carey was merely the point of the sword. Through his servant, God unleashed the greatest missionary thrust the church had ever seen, and it would carry the gospel to every part of the globe.

Christ's Kingdom Advances

Carey's watchword took on physical form in the nineteenth century—the century of missions. Beginning in the late 1700s, scores of mission agencies were formed, many of them the result of cooperation among evangelical denominations. From them, thousands of missionaries poured forth, moving like a mighty army into India, China, sub-Saharan Africa, and the islands of the Pacific. They willingly suffered great deprivation and hardship for the cause of Christ.

My grandparents were part of that movement, leaving the United States to labor as missionaries in the high mountains of Bolivia. My grandmother miscarried twin girls (and nearly lost her own life) as a result of typhoid fever. While she lay incoherent, my grandfather delivered the babies using only a primitive surgeon's kit. Such events were commonplace on the mission field, and were generally borne with great patience for Christ's sake. Despite such hardships, the gospel went out in power; God's elect were called to faith; and indigenous churches were established around the world.

In the twentieth century, the horrors of war, repression, and genocide only served to strengthen the church worldwide. Once again, a multitude of unknown missionaries shared the gospel in prisons, in death camps, and on the battlefield. Communism barred missionaries from much of the East, but it could not stop the gospel. Eastern Europe is now hungry for the truth, and China has an indigenous church that is growing by nearly thirty thousand souls every day! Reports from Central and South America show that a spiritually moribund Roman Catholicism is giving way to living, growing, evangelistic churches. And Africa, once called "the missionary's graveyard," is in the midst of a revival that is birthing four hundred new churches a week! Christ's kingdom is advancing, and we can foresee a day—not too far away—when truly "the earth will be full of the knowledge of the LORD as the waters cover the sea" (Isa. 11:9).

No More Fear

The fear of something like gunfire is nothing compared to the excitement of sharing God's truth. God has chosen to use people like you and me to bring the good news of salvation to the nations. And when we do that, whether next door or in Africa, we become the agents of God's eternal purposes.

Young man, as a believer, you are a part of his plan to call the nations to faith. Through missions, you can be involved in something of inestimable value—something that fulfills your desire to do something great. God gave you this desire so that you could spend it in his service. Where will he use you? I don't know. But begin now to plan for that day, and be ready to go wherever he leads you. Expect great things from God; attempt great things for God.

Prayer Resolves

- To pray regularly for the extension of Christ's kingdom and for those who serve as missionaries in countries around the world—especially those supported by my church
- To find practical ways to become part of the worldwide work of missions right where I am
- To support the work of missions by giving regularly
- To become a missionary at home, being ready to answer the call of God, whenever and wherever he may send me

Scripture Memory

"All authority in heaven and on earth has been given to me. Therefore go and make disciples of all nations, baptizing them in the name of the Father and of the Son and of the Holy Spirit, and teaching them to obey everything I have commanded you. And surely I am with you always, to the very end of the age."

Matthew 28:18–20

For Discussion

1. In order to become a missionary, what changes (both adding and subtracting) must I make in my lifestyle?
2. Why would God place the desire to do something great in the heart of every young man? How does God define greatness?
3. What is it about the character of the gospel that makes Christians want to share it with others? What does this tell you about those who don't?

"How Sweet and Awful Is the Place"

Pity the nations, O our God!
Constrain the earth to come;
Send thy victorious Word abroad,
And bring the strangers home.

We long to see thy churches full,
That all the chosen race
May with one voice, and heart and soul,
Sing thy redeeming grace.

Isaac Watts, 1707

For Further Study

A History of Christian Missions, by Stephen Neill; *The Diary of David Brainerd*; *How the Irish Saved Civilization*, by Thomas Cahill; *From Jerusalem to Irian Jaya*, by Ruth Tucker; *Operation World*, by Patrick Johnstone; *Let the Nations Be Glad*, by John Piper; *A History of Christianity*, by Kenneth Scott Latourette

YOUNG MEN: CULTURE AND ART

9

CULTURE AND WARFARE

Hebrews 11

Retreat!

How would you answer the question: What is the biggest problem in the church today? A Christian I know replied without a hint of hesitation, "Cultural retreatism."

What is cultural retreatism, you ask? The short answer: Cultural retreatism happens when Christians retreat into a subculture that loses meaningful connection with, and influence in, society and culture. Think Amish. Usually folks who use the term are referring to how few Christians excel as mainstream artists, musicians, movie directors, authors, poets, journalists, and politicians. Finally, if cultural retreatism is the vice to shun, the virtue to embrace is cultural engagement.

Of course, Christians have shrunk from their responsibility to be salt and light at various times in history and in a variety of ways. But is it the *biggest* problem? I'm concerned that if it isn't, but we insist that it is, we might find ourselves, as C. S. Lewis put it, "running about with fire extinguishers whenever there is a flood." Let me illustrate.

While teaching writing to teenagers, I have observed a pattern. Students try to improve their writing by using big words and affecting a sophisticated style. This has never improved anyone's writing. What is more, it becomes a superficial way of hiding the real problem. Elisabeth Elliot perceptively advised young writers: "Never aim at style; aim at authenticity."

I fear that when we define the biggest problem in the church as cultural retreatism, it sets us up to make the same mistake my writing students make when they aim for style. The result easily becomes a scrambling after intellectual acceptance and artistic credibility; in short, we can become contortionists, bending over backward to legitimize—in the eyes of the world and her experts—the Christian gospel.

Still worse, grasping after cultural engagement can lead to compromise, to giving up some ground—on nonessentials, at first—by which we hope to be a sophisticated voice in the discussion.

Cultural retreatism reminds me of military tactical language. When the battle is going against an army, they have several options. They might cut their losses and retreat, in hopes of fighting again. They might lay down their arms and surrender. They might make peace. They might submit to conquest and become slaves of the conquerors. Or they might fight to the death.

Engagement is also a military term. A fighting term. You and I are in a war. And yes, engaging the culture is an important part of our duties as Christians. But rightly engaging the culture is a bloody business, and historically, it has been the Christians who have done the bleeding.

Commended for What?

The writer of the book of Hebrews describes a bloody litany of Christian persecution down through the centuries: from jeering, to stoning, to being sawed in two. He commends a noble host of saints who walked by faith when the world hated them and "persecuted and mistreated" them for it. No wonder he concludes "the world was not worthy of them" (Heb. 11:37–38).

But when you hear things like this it sounds a bit odd. When was the last time you worried about being sawed in two for your faith? When were you last ridiculed for being a Christian? Take your time. Dredge something up. The truth is, few of us have any experience that sounds anything like what you've just read from Hebrews.

But if you lived in Indonesia today, where teenage girls have been beheaded for their faith in Christ, and teenage young men have been arrested and beaten for attending a Christian worship service, this would not sound the least bit odd.

Or if you lived in China and your father had just been hauled away to prison for preaching at a house church, and you knew that it was unlikely that you'd ever see him again; or if you lived in the Sudan and Islamic fundamentalists had just burned down your house and killed your parents before your eyes, and you were on a death march with a band of other Christian boys, hunted, hungry, and terrified by the ugly reality of it all—if your life were like theirs, none of what you have just read in Hebrews would sound the least bit odd.

When Jesus Calls a Man . . .

All this moves us closer to answering the original question: What is the biggest problem in the church today? It may be that in all our efforts to engage the culture and the world around us, the church has actually surrendered to the culture, laid down its arms, capitulated to the enemy, and, worse yet, become her slaves. If that is the case, cultural retreatism, real as it is, would be a far lesser crime than cultural engagement run amuck. Cultural engagement in the Bible demanded total commitment to Christ, whatever the cost—something that Christians seem a bit fuzzy about today.

Dietrich Bonhoeffer understood that his walk with Christ could very well cost him everything. He wrote, "When Jesus calls a man, he bids him come and die." Bonhoeffer was forced to decide between following Adolf Hitler and following Christ; his choice cost him his life, as it had for the heroes described in Hebrews 11, as it had for countless saints in the early church, as it had for eighteen thousand Scottish Covenanters in the seventeenth century, as it does for thousands of nameless brethren throughout the world today.

Jesus said, "If anyone would come after me, he must deny himself and take up his cross and follow me" (Matt. 16:24). Following Christ is a costly business, a bloody business, and one that many American young men find much too difficult and not nearly as appealing as following the world. For many, cultural engagement can easily descend into simply another way—a sophisticated way—of disguising worldliness. The result of such self-deception can be an arrogant besmirching of Christ and a belittling of the gospel.

Two Parallel Lives

I wonder if C. S. Lewis did not cut to the heart of the biggest problem in his immortal *Screwtape Letters*. In it, his senior tempter Screwtape advises his nephew Wormwood how to secure his patient's soul for hell by playing on just such a self-deception, by nudging him toward a pseudo-pious invincibility when it comes to worldly friends and influences:

> If he is a big enough fool, he can be induced to live, for quite long periods, two parallel lives. He can be made to take positive pleasure in the perception that the two sides of his life are inconsistent. This is done by exploiting his vanity. He can be taught to enjoy kneeling beside the grocer on Sunday just because he remembers that the grocer could not possibly understand the urbane and mocking world which he inhabited on Saturday evening;

and contrariwise, to enjoy the bawdy and blasphemy over coffee with these admirable friends all the more because he is aware of a "deeper" "spiritual" world within him which they cannot understand. You see the idea—the worldly friends touch him on the one side and the grocer on the other, and he is the complete, balanced, complex man who sees round them all. Thus, he will feel, instead of shame, a continual undercurrent of self-satisfaction. Finally, you can persuade him, in defiance of conscience, that he is, in some unspecific way, doing these people "good" by the mere fact of drinking their cocktails and laughing at their jokes, and that to cease to do so would be "priggish," "intolerant" and (of course) "Puritanical."

Put yourself in the place of the one being tempted here. It should not be too difficult. If you're like me, you're also a "big enough fool" to be taken in by this sophisticated, foot-in-both-worlds posture. Perhaps this is such a big problem because by falling into the devil's scheme in this way, we actually spin the resulting worldliness into spiritual superiority. Instead of being mortified with shame at our folly, we feel smug and self-satisfied with ourselves for our cultural engagement.

Let me illustrate this brand of cultural engagement with an interview I read in a leading Christian magazine about a rocker who calls himself a Christian, who got started playing music in British invasion cover bands and power-pop combos, after which he toured for ten years in a band that opened concerts for the Beach Boys.

The interviewer asked the compelling question whether "anything ever came up in [his] decade with the band to make [him] question [his] decision to be a part of secular bands."

The Christian rocker replied:

I never questioned it. I could go from the Christian, church-going, never-say-a-bad-word-about-anyone table to the I-only-smoke-dope-and-occa-sionally-snort-coke-and-play-in-bars table. I could cross from one to the other and feel totally comfortable in either setting. And while the Christian table was frowning on me, I reminded them—not that I was Christ—that Christ said, "Why are you hanging out with your own people when you should be ministering to the other people?" [He laughs.] I wasn't always perfect, but I like to think that I had some kind of an influence. And I'm still good friends with everyone in the Beach Boys."

He concluded by expressing that God had blessed him "by allowing me to meet and play with so many of the people I've been influenced by."

Take a moment and reread the paragraph from Lewis quoted above that begins, "If he is a big enough fool." It almost sounds as though someone made up the Christian rocker's rationale as a parody of precisely what Lewis was warning against. Only Lewis's "doing these people 'good' " declines into the even more subjective "I like to think that I had some kind of an influence." Some kind of influence? What would first-century evangelism have looked like if Paul or Peter had taken this approach? Obviously, this man's brand of cultural engagement didn't earn him the scorn of the world (or was he blissfully unaware of it?), much less the persecution described in Hebrews 11. I don't get the sense from reading Hebrews that these heroes felt "totally comfortable" with the world. Was Jesus "totally comfortable" with the first-century Roman or Jewish world?

At the beginning of this rocker's Beach Boys–influenced album collection, ironically he quotes C. S. Lewis: "The whole of man is to drink joy from the fountain of joy." Curious, isn't it, how much we prefer picking and choosing when it comes to Lewis or, worse yet, Holy Scripture. The Westminster divines summarized the Bible's teaching regarding the chief end of man: we are "to glorify God and to enjoy him forever." Enjoyment without glorifying God, however, leads to shameless self-deception. Glorifying is expressed in holiness of life— and holiness, like it or not (the children of Israel often did not), means being set apart from the world.

Roaring Lions

What does the Bible say? "Friendship with the world is hatred toward God," the apostle James wrote (4:4). Israel always got herself into trouble when she failed to keep herself separate from unbelieving Canaan, when she failed to drive out the inhabitants of the Promised Land, when she failed to put to death everyone and everything under the ban, when she engaged the culture around her. And so do you.

But doesn't the Bible also say that we are to be all things to all people, to be in the world but not of the world? I wonder if these would not have been Lot's favorite proof texts. Let's be honest. Nine times out of ten, when you and I raise these objections we are merely looking for ways to legitimize our worldliness. Again, it is curious how these texts tip the scales and effectively silence the clear and relentless cautions stretching throughout the pages of the Bible. A wise young man must not be deceived by these arguments.

If those who identify cultural retreatism as the biggest problem in the church were right, I would suggest that passages such as those that command us to "come out from them and be separate" (2 Cor. 6:17) would read, "Go to them and engage their culture," or "be friends with the world and so fulfill the law of Christ." Yet that is not how the Bible reads.

You, young man, are in a life-or-death combat, in a battle, in an engagement for your immortal soul. Or you ought to be. And your enemies—the world, the flesh, and the devil—hover all about you. The devil, the quintessential deceiver, loves the apparent tension created by these two poles of obedience, of being "in the world but not of the world." He wants you to cross the line all the time, to think that you are the well-rounded, balanced guy who is uniquely able to be "totally comfortable" in both worlds, to be salt and light, to be culturally relevant, hip, with it, cool, loved by the world because you, like few others, have achieved the ultimate balance, able to move from either table, to be "good friends with everyone" in the world and with her popular cultural icons.

Fight-to-the-Death Watchfulness

Don't be a fool. Organize your spiritual life around cultural engagement and you will in all likelihood aim either at pop-culture hip or at sophistication. Beware. You may find yourself a proud lover of the world and the things of the world and, at the last, an enemy of God.

If you are to engage and reform your culture, you must first learn to think and act like a Christian man who lives in a desperately sinful world, a Christian man who watches the path of his feet, who knows his vulnerability, who arms himself for that engagement, who bends every fiber of his being against the enemy, and who knows that with worldliness the best defense is, as Victorian preacher C. H. Spurgeon put it, "a good pair of legs and the King's Highway." You must flee youthful lusts, and so you must flee from every worldly influence that would make it easier for you to sin. Some might call this cultural retreatism. But only a fool ridicules biblical watchfulness. Preferring cultural engagement to fight-to-the-death watchfulness puts you off your guard and makes you accepting and uncritical of worldly influences. People like that lose the war and end up slaves.

Peter put it this way: "Be self-controlled and alert. Your enemy the devil prowls around like a roaring lion looking for someone to devour. Resist him, standing firm in the faith" (1 Peter 5:8–9). Paul put it this way: "Do not conform any longer to the pattern of this world, but be transformed by the renewing of your mind" (Rom. 12:2).

Christians who set about to engage the culture may find themselves so fearful of the world's contempt as they engage the culture, so desperate not to be foolish as they're so sure other Christians have been, so busy trying to make Christianity acceptable to society by not offending non-Christians, that their cultural engagement gradually looks less and less like anything that resembles true Christianity.

"History has shown that when society embraces religion," wrote one cultural critic, "religion usually hugs back. Accommodation is often followed by assimilation and amalgamation. We accept some popularity and, craving more, we discard the convictions we have that might be unpopular." At the last, "our identity as Christians is threatened."

If history has shown this, then our biggest problem is accommodation and conformity to the world and culture, our preference for worldly things over heavenly ones. Ironically, the good intentions of many who are deeply concerned about cultural engagement can perversely lead to capitulation to the very culture they sincerely wanted to engage.

And it all happens so gradually, with such stealth and subtlety, that you may find yourself so under the influence of the world that you can no longer hear the folly of your own rationalization: "I could cross from one to the other and feel totally comfortable in either setting." At the last, you may be so befuddled that you bless God for allowing you "to meet and play with so many of the people" who have influenced you. If you live arm-in-arm with culture, it won't even occur to you that cultural engagement was supposed to be about you influencing culture, instead of the reverse.

Don't lay down your arms and surrender to the culture. This is war. Join the heroes of faith. Master your weapons. Hold your ground. Keep your eyes fixed on Jesus, not on the world. Then fight to the death.

Prayer Resolves

- To keep my eyes first on Jesus, not on the world and the culture
- To keep my Bible open, preferring it to worldly, sophisticated wisdom
- To be unashamed of the gospel
- Not to capitulate to the culture, not even an inch
- To engage the world with total commitment to Christ

Scripture Memory

"Be self-controlled and alert. Your enemy the devil prowls around like a roaring lion looking for someone to devour. Resist him, standing firm in the faith."

1 Peter 5:8–9a

For Discussion

1. What are ways in which you have heard others rationalize their worldliness?
2. What are ways in which you rationalize your own worldliness?

3. Discuss what the Bible does mean when it tells us to be in the world but not of the world.

4. Discuss how Daniel, Joseph, Moses, David, and others became so influential in their cultures. Was it by a calculated plan to engage the culture, or was it by standing against the cultural tide, faithfully obeying God?

"The Lord, Great Sovereign"

God's blessed, redeemed, and chosen ones,
     His children shout and sing!
"All praise to Christ, the Cornerstone,
     Triumphant, glorious King!"

Douglas Bond, 2001

For Further Study

Genesis 41:37–57; Exodus 6:28–7:7

10

CULTURE, WORLDLINESS, AND CHRIST

1 Corinthians 1:18–31

"Just" Saved

I have benefited greatly from reading books challenging me to have a Christian worldview and from attending courses and visiting study centers that have urged me to be salt and light in an unsavory and dark world. In short, I have benefited from instruction that challenged me to engage the culture.

But there is a potential danger here. Reading an article reviewing highlights of one such seminar recently, I was forced to reread what one exuberant young man said after attending. "I was always taught," he said, "that Christianity was just about how to get saved and have a relationship with God. I never learned that it had anything to do with politics, science, the arts . . . This course has opened up a whole new world for me!"

Clearly, it's a good thing when a young man realizes that all of life is sacred and to be lived to the glory of God, including politics, science, and the arts. But what disturbed me about this young man's euphoria was that getting saved and having a relationship with God—the most stupendous gifts in all the world—after a course on engaging culture, just didn't seem like much. When being forgiven takes a backseat to engaging the culture in politics, science, and art, the problem is no longer potential—it is tragically real.

Tom Sawyer concluded that "Sunday School ain't shucks to a circus." And it seems that we may be in danger of concluding that the foolishness of the cross ain't shucks to cultural engagement. The redemption of our souls from death and hell no longer opened up a new world for this young man, but cultural engagement did. How unlike the four women John Bunyan overheard who spoke about salvation and Christ "as if they had found a new world."

God Chose Fools

Reading Paul's first letter to Corinth, one concludes that their biggest problem was worldliness. And I fear that today's church is a great deal more like the Corinthian church than we care to admit. Like them, we prefer the world's wisdom over God's. We want to believe that somehow our witness can be sophisticated in the eyes of the world and are particularly averse to sneers of contempt from the intellectual world. We cringe when people such as Oxford atheist Richard Dawkins dismiss Christians as "unsophisticates and children," and scramble to prove him wrong.

We want to distance ourselves from the anti-intellectualism of the fundamentalists. We're convinced that their Christianity was childish, even foolish, but ours is cultured, philosophical, grown-up, even sophisticated. As a result, Christian doctrine, worship, piety, service, and witness are being redefined—and taking heavy casualties in the process.

In *The Confessions*, St. Augustine candidly admitted that as a young scholar he had loved worldly wisdom, classical philosophy and literature, and the praise of men. He confessed that the Scriptures "appeared to [him] to be unworthy," that his "inflated pride shunned her style." He looked with contempt on the Bible and dismissed it as a child's book, intended for "little ones, but [he] scorned to be a little one. Swollen with pride," wrote Augustine, "I looked upon myself as a great one."

You feel the pull; I know you do. You keep quiet about being a Christian in certain company because it just isn't cool. But Paul hits the mark. The root of the problem is that we forget the sovereignty of God in our own salvation and in that of the lost. We forget that "God chose the foolish things of the world to shame the wise; God chose the weak things of the world to shame the strong. He chose the lowly things of this world and the despised things—and the things that are not—to nullify the things that are, so that no one may boast before him" (1 Cor. 1:27–29).

But you and I don't like being fools, being weak, being despised. We don't like being nobody. As a young man, you want to be great and take pride in your own wisdom. You want to boast of great things. So did Paul's audience at Corinth, and so does the church today. As a result, Christians are entirely too busy wringing our hands over what the world thinks of us. We want to be wise in the world's eyes. This sets us up to surrender a great deal to the so-called wisdom of our culture. It's time for us to wake up and confess that we justify a good deal of this surrendering in the name of cultural engagement.

Coward!

We should know better. Paul's warning is not unique in the pages of Holy Scripture. Repeatedly we are warned against the urge to compromise with worldly wisdom. In 1984, in his last public address before his death, Christian apologist Francis Schaeffer did not declare cultural retreatism the biggest problem for the church at the end of the twentieth century. Rather, he expressed threefold fear that the church would sink into "accommodation, accommodation, accommodation."

When the church accommodates the culture, it is simply another way of capitulating, of surrendering, of giving up all resistance and acquiescing to the culture. Given the Bible's relentless charge for you to do the opposite—to stand fast, to resist, to watch, to be on your guard, to hold fast, and not to conform to the world—Dr. Schaeffer's reply seems more on the mark than the reply of some who claim to hold the sophisticated high ground in Christian cultural engagement.

Few would disagree that judges engage the culture, that they wield enormous influence in our legal, cultural, and political life. I wonder what Justice Antonin Scalia would call the biggest problem for Christians today. Surely a judge in our nation's highest court would urge other Christians to engage the culture as he is doing. But listen to Justice Scalia's charge: "Have the courage to have your wisdom regarded as stupidity. Be fools for Christ. And have the courage to suffer the contempt of the sophisticated world."

Notice that he doesn't urge you to aim at engaging the culture, to aim at being an artist, moviemaker, journalist, judge, or politician, or to play in a rock 'n' roll band. He tells you something very different. And what he tells you requires you to stand against the culture. Aim at cultural engagement and you will be reluctant to be a fool for Christ. After all, being a fool is not very sophisticated, and nobody likes being called weak and stupid.

Justice Scalia's remarks should help us own up to the central problem for Christians today. We prefer the worldly-wise man, the scholar, "the philosopher of this age," to the contempt of Christ and his gospel. I wonder if this is not why we've done more surrendering to the culture than engaging it in any transforming way. We lack "the courage to suffer the contempt of the sophisticated world." We've been spiritual cowards. We fear the contempt of the world more than we fear God.

Friends with the Enemy

What results is a tragicomedy, with Christians groping about, trying to legitimize their faith in the eyes of the world. Desperate to have our faith appear relevant to the world, we conform our worship to the appetites of the culture and create seeker-friendly churches, ones that look and sound more like self-help encounter gatherings, or that surrender so much to the culture they look and sound more like nightlife at The Sands Hotel in Las Vegas, a Hollywood celebrity gala, or a hyped-up multilevel sales convention. Or perhaps more like Tom Sawyer's circus.

Capitulation to worldly methods in our church services is based on a theological shift away from Paul's emphasis on the sovereignty of God in salvation. Aping the entertainment culture, we depend far more on our culturally engaging services than on the foundation of God's sovereignty in salvation, the bedrock truth that man becomes a Christian by an act of God, not by high-octane, emotionally charged music, movie clips, jokes, and glitz, or by any other well-intentioned tactics of postconservative evangelicalism.

Perhaps worse, Christians more in tune with the historical and theological origins of their faith scorn the pop culture and aim at creating an intellectual-friendly environment, a sophisticated Christianity, a cerebral Christianity, a Christianity for the successful and well-to-do, for the well-educated, a sort of country-club, highbrow, Ivy League Christianity. Christianity with snob appeal. Paul would never have put up with this capitulation, either. Paul's message was not delivered "with wise and persuasive words, but with a demonstration of the Spirit's power, so that your faith might not rest on men's wisdom, but on God's power" (1 Cor. 2:4–5).

Christians who venerate modern scholarship, who engage in what a friend of mine calls "Ph.D. worship," who assume that worldly scholars are trustworthy, inevitably find themselves giving up some ground to what modern science tells us about origins, or what archaeologists tell us about ancient Near Eastern civilization, or what the experts tell us we are to believe about biblical accounts of supernatural events. Once ground has been relinquished, it is rarely regained. Usually more is lost. It's curious that the world's scholars rarely budge an inch. It's Christians who are supposed to do all the fudging. And what we don't surrender now (count on it), you and your children will in the next generation.

Designer Tents

How different all of this is from the faith of the Christian heroes celebrated in Hebrews 11. By showing contempt for the wisdom of the sophisticated world, they honored Christ and suffered "the contempt of the sophisticated world," and paid the ultimate price for it. This takes courage, Christian courage, manly courage. The easy path is spiritual cowardice, but we'd never call it that. Call it sophisticated cultural engagement, call it "being all things to all people," call it "when in Rome do as the Romans do," call it anything but what it so often is—spiritual cowardice.

Imagine how different Paul's witness to the world would have been if he had aimed for cultural engagement. He would have set up a study center in the mountains of Greece and invited artists and thinkers from Athens to come and sip tree-pitch wine with him and discuss philosophy. Or maybe he would have worked his way into politics, or taken up painting, or the lyre and started a band, or maybe become a cultural analyst. Perhaps he would have come up with designer tents and hosted trade shows where connoisseurs of the latest fashions in tent design would gather to gush at what Paul was capable of doing with camel hair.

Creative John Bunyan never wrote a word about cultural engagement, but he profoundly influenced his culture. How did he do it? It was in part by winsomely illustrating the biblical posture that a young man should have toward the world. In his immortal *Pilgrim's Progress*, in the first scene in the House of the Interpreter, Bunyan describes a picture of a man with his "eyes lifted up to heaven, the best of books in his hand, the law of truth written upon his lips, the world behind his back." Here is the biblical posture for a Christian young man. How do you lead others? With your back to them, showing them the way to Christ and eternal life, pointing the way to truth by leadership. Furthermore, throughout his journey, Christian was at his best when he was watchful, on guard, his sword drawn, his feet not straying from the King's Highway. So it is with you and me.

I fear that organizing your life around cultural engagement as conceived today will switch things around. In place of the best of books, you will have a book of worldly philosophy in your hands and your arms overflowing with the world's toys. This subtly develops into the idea that in order to demolish the world's arguments, it is more important for you to master their philosophies, their art, their music, their movies—instead of mastering the Bible.

Witness over the Rail

In 1980 I began reading books on Christian apologetics and decided that I needed to know more about existentialism. Fair enough. Then I went abroad to learn more at a Christian study center. Gradually, a layer of dust settled on my Bible. Meanwhile, I learned heaps about art, culture, and the world's philosophy. In fact, I learned so much of the world's philosophy that I was pretty sure other Christians—you know, the simpleminded ones—were pretty clueless about the larger issues of culture.

I had become a "thinking Christian." Meanwhile, more layers of dust settled on my Bible. Soon it was virtually a closed book. Especially silent were such parts as Paul in today's reading: "Has not God made foolish the wisdom of the world?"(1 Cor. 1:20). If someone quoted Scripture at mealtime discussions in order to apply it to the topic under consideration, the thinking Christians at the table exchanged pitying glances. Someone would usually clear his throat and condescendingly suggest that proof texts from the Bible were rarely helpful in thoughtful discussions.

Eager to engage the culture in a sophisticated fashion, I went through a period of dutifully remaining silent about my faith. I needed to listen, and listen some more. When I had finally learned enough about modern, or postmodern, or post-postmodern philosophy, then I'd be able to offer a clever answer.

All the while, I nearly lost my grip of the truth Paul here expressed that "the message of the cross is foolishness to those who are perishing," that "it is because of [God's choice] that you are in Christ Jesus," that "the world through its wisdom did not know [God]," that "God was pleased through the foolishness of what was preached to save those who believe" (1 Cor. 1:18, 30, 21). How sly the devil is! He can distort or silence our witness and make us think we're being wise in doing so—and creative and sophisticated in the bargain.

Moreover, when you calculate your engagement of the culture by the appetites of the culture, you'll be tempted to pick and choose Christian doctrine. There's offensive stuff in the Bible. The church-growth experts insist that offensive doctrines will drive the lost away. So what truths are first over the rail? Total depravity and the sovereignty of God, that "God chose the foolish things . . . so that no one may boast" (1 Cor. 1:27–29). Prefer the wisdom of the world, fear giving offense, grope after relevance, fear driving the world away, and at the last, truth will be mute, the devil glad—and hell will be kicking up its heels.

Boast in Christ

I recently read an interview with a Hollywood horror-film producer—a Christian one: "Being a faithful Christian in Hollywood," he concluded, "is about making excellent movies." That's it? Think what would have happened to Western culture if Peter had said the equivalent: "Being a faithful Christian in Galilee is about being an excellent fisherman." Or Matthew: "Being a faithful Christian in Jerusalem is about being an excellent tax collector." Or Bunyan: "Being a Christian in Bedford is about being an excellent tinker."

Certainly Christians have different callings and are to fulfill those callings with excellence. But in our entertainment-crazed culture, to lionize Christians who make "excellent movies," or play excellent music or football, or paint what the experts tell us are excellent pictures, will produce a generation of pussyfoot Christians with the equivalent of spiritual duct tape over their mouths—though, you can be sure, it will be designer duct tape worn with style.

Aiming at cultural engagement is like aiming at making yourself happy; neither aim hits its mark. The person who is absorbed in making himself happy never is. The young man who is absorbed in cultural engagement never does. Worse yet, Paul suggests that a preoccupation with worldly wisdom will make you boastful, but it won't be about Christ that you're boasting.

Joseph rose to unimaginable influence by living a holy life, by rigorous piety, by keeping himself unstained by worldly Egypt—not by setting out to engage culture. So it was with Daniel, Moses, Peter, and the great cloud of witnesses celebrated for their faith. So it will be with you.

Stop aiming at cultural engagement. Aim at Christ. Aim at holiness, at being set apart from the world, at being a fool for Christ. Stop boasting about your engagement with worldly wisdom. Boast in Christ. Then ready yourself for the scorn and the derision of the world. Brace yourself. It will come. Be confident, however, that on the great day the world's wisdom will be unmasked as the real foolishness. So stop caring about the world's contempt. Say with John Newton, "Let the world deride or pity, I will glory in thy Name." Engage the enemy. Be a friend of God. Boast in Christ.

Prayer Resolves

- To know more of Christ and his Word than of the world and its wisdom
- To view my calling and gifts not as ends but as means
- To make maximum use of my calling now and in the future for the glory of God and the progress of Christ's kingdom
- Not to fear the contempt of the world
- Not to capitulate to worldly wisdom or make peace with the culture

Scripture Memory

"Anyone who chooses to be a friend of the world becomes an enemy of God."

James 4:4

For Discussion

1. List influential Christians and discuss how they rose to prominence. Compare their lives and influence with influential men in the Bible.
2. What activity that you want to be involved in would you try to justify by labeling as "cultural engagement"?
3. How might this activity turn you more toward the world and its wisdom and away from Christ and his Word?
4. Discuss whether you need to alter your thinking about this activity or whether you need to alter your involvement in it.

"Glorious Things of Thee Are Spoken"

Fading is the worldling's pleasure,
All his boasted pomp and show,
Solid joys and lasting pleasures,
None but Zion's children know.

John Newton, 1779

For Further Study

Daniel 6; Acts 17:16–34

11

THE DEATH OF ART

Psalm 27

Meaningless Goodness?

More than twenty years ago, I ducked out of a San Francisco rain shower into a doorway—as it turned out, the doorway to a steep staircase leading up five flights to an artist's loft. I entered and saw the strangest sight.

One entire wall was spanned by a wooden frame stretched with a canvas. But not just any canvas. This one was a clever hodgepodge of old clothes: jeans, T-shirts, overalls, zippers, buttons, and snaps—a sort of grab-bag, thrift-store canvas. I watched in amazement as the artist smeared paint on his canvas, dipping randomly from a variety of paint cans.

"Unusual canvas," I ventured at last.

"Pretty cool, huh?" he replied, grinning at me over his shoulder as he continued to apply paint with a large brush.

After several moments of chat about his creation, I asked if his artwork was didactic.

"Di—what?" he replied.

I tried again. "Does it mean something?"

"Mean something?" he snorted, flicking a wet brush at a pair of paint-stiffened trousers. "Of course it doesn't mean anything. Life doesn't mean anything."

"So why do you bother doing it?"

"Because I'm good at it."

Curious about the criteria he used to come to this absolutist conclusion, I probed further. How could life be meaningless and he be good or bad at anything? If it was meaningless, wouldn't it be impossible to measure goodness or badness? He frowned.

Believing that life doesn't mean anything, after all, is an evaluative perspective, a belief. As C. S. Lewis observed, "If the whole universe has no meaning, we should never have found out that it has no meaning." Thus, by denying that life means anything, he unwittingly admitted that meaning does exist—absolutely. If it didn't, we would never have had the discussion, nor would he bother creating art that attempts to mirror his nihilistic philosophy of life. At this point, the intricacies of his painting seemed to require more of his concentration. So I left.

Art as Religion

In the same breath that many artists and academics declare that there are no absolutes, they say things like this: "Art is a means of giving order to the chaos of experience." "Art represents the source of human values." "Art gives meaning to life." The cultural editor for *WORLD* magazine, Gene Edward Veith, suggests that these statements are various ways of placing "art and the artist squarely in the position of God—as creator, lawgiver, and redeemer."

Listen to almost any artist or art critic speak about art, and you will hear the terminology of religion: *creation, inspiration, transcen-*

dence, vision. In this pseudo-religious milieu, artists are the high priests, works of art are the equivalent of relics, the elite appreciators are the worshipers, the adulations uttered are the responses prescribed in the liturgy, taxes to support artists are the forced tithes, grand museums are the temples, and the baffled masses scratching our heads are the equivalent of the heathen unbelievers. Absurdly, all of this in a world that demands a separation of church and state!

The resulting "chronological snobbery," as C. S. Lewis dubbed it, can have the effect of making you feel unsophisticated, a sort of aesthetic atheist. You may begin to feel as though your worldview is out of touch, not very intellectual. You may even be tempted to feel ashamed of being a Christian. At the end of the day, however, all of this is merely another form of idolatry, another way of putting something else in place of the grandeur of truth and making truth look silly. It takes first-rate deception to pull it off, but then, that's what the devil is so good at.

Laws Governing Freedom in Art

There is one constant for the Christian young man trying to sort out what he is to think about art: artistic fashion changes constantly. Ironically, as artists speak in religious terms about their art, a form of self-worship, they venerate something that is inherently changing, something that in a very short time will be sneered at by the next generation of artistic gurus.

"Art reflects the temper of its culture," wrote Gene Edward Veith. And a culture that is constantly being shaped and reformed by the transient appetites of people groping for the next amusement, for the next entertainment thrill, for the latest technology, for the newest fashion in clothes—or music, or cars, or coffee—will produce art that reflects these flighty, laser-light-show changes.

Still, there is another unchangeable law among the artistic elite: the more innovative, the better. This rigid law leads immediately to another: the more bizarre, the more shocking, the more valuable the art.

Art in a Culture of Death

Perhaps there is no better example of this than the sensational "death art" of German doctor Gunther von Hagen, who has developed a technique whereby he can turn human tissue into plastic and shape corpses into "art." With the help of his father, a retired Nazi SS sergeant, Hagen set up a plastination factory in Poland where on his father's last visit he sent sixty human beings to death camps during the war.

Hagen's art features a dead man riding a skinned horse, the man's corpse positioned holding both the horse's brain and his own. It gets much worse. With the aid of U.S. taxpayers, human corpses, skinned and contorted into grotesque lifelike, sometimes provocative poses, have created a freaky sensation in American art and science museums. Since 1997, Hagen's "Body Works" art has been viewed by seventeen million museumgoers, including thousands of schoolchildren, raking in some two hundred million dollars in the bargain.

For the Christian, this should not be a close call. In Holy Scripture we are taught that our bodies are not our own, that they are temples of the living God. When man made in the image of God dies, his body is to be buried, there to await the resurrection of the body; it is not to be burned, mutilated, or desecrated—not even in the all-excusing name of art. Hagen's morbid creations seem to epitomize what Gene Edward Veith calls "art in the culture of death."

Beauty and the Beholder

A former student, frustrated at the ugliness all around him while deployed onboard ship during the global war on terror, e-mailed me with questions about art and beauty. He wrote: "Being surrounded by the people I have been around for the last few months has started my mind on a question. What makes some people capable of enjoying beauty and others not? Why am I able to enjoy literature, poetry, and J. S. Bach and my shipmates are not? Secondly, what makes something beautiful? I know we talked about this in high school. I'm ashamed to say that I probably wasn't paying good enough attention, but I was hoping for a refresher."

My reply: "Confusion results when postmoderns shape the argument by insisting that everything, including beauty, is simply a matter of taste: like favorite flavors of ice cream. It is critical to their argument that there be no universal qualities of beauty. Their insistence notwithstanding, beauty is not in the eye of the beholder. Though art seems subjective, any thoughtful Christian is reality-bound to disagree with the elitists here. Why? Because there are universal noncultural, nonethnic agreements about beauty.

"Few would attempt to disagree that all peoples, wherever they are in the continuum of civilization, find beauty in a sunset, in a mother tenderly caring for a newborn, the vastness of the ocean, the music of the breaking surf, sunlight sparkling on a mountain lake, the soaring of an eagle—all this creates a sublime wonder in everyone regardless of culture, ethnicity, or gender. The things that are truly beautiful imitate the parts of our world less tainted by the fall, or they create a sense of longing for those things. When art features sin, it ought to be in a way that unmasks fallenness for what it is. In the end, all true art is redemptive; it lifts us above the base things and gives us a longing for the perfections of heaven.

"So why do the guys on the ship not appreciate Bach and other beautiful things? One explanation is that they have been so bent by pop culture and the need for immediate gratification that they have no appetite for transcendent beautiful things. They are enslaved to immediate and tactile gratification in the music they listen to, the pornography they devour, and the games and videos to which they have made themselves willing slaves.

"Real beauty represented in fine art lifts us out of ourselves, elevates us above our desires for twisted gratification, and shows us a glimmer of what a world would be like if it were not wrenched from its original design into something barbaric and crude.

129

Hell on the Ship

"It is all very tragic, Stuart. The people on your ship are lost, and their indifference to or disdain for true beauty is simply an expression of their lostness. I hope this will deepen your compassion for them and your appreciation for a mother who introduced you to art and beauty when you were very young. Moreover, I hope it will create a deeper longing for heaven and eternity where all that is bent and ugly—the rap, pornography, drunkenness—will vanish and Bach and Rembrandt—and a host of other great artists—will be loved by all!

"The fact that beauty has survived, even in our fallen world, is further demonstration of the truly great artists' eternal conception of beauty. Perhaps Bach has outlived the vicissitudes of the centuries because he struck the chord of eternity in his music. His is music that must endure. And what's true of music must also be true of visual art and the rest. Raunchy, throwaway music, like raunchy visual art, twists goodness out of shape and then celebrates the deformity instead of the eternal beauties.

"The pounding ugliness of what your shipmates listen to does not strike the chord of eternity, perhaps because what they prefer has broken the instrument with chaos and a celebration of all that is unworthy. Unworthy and ugly, it celebrates not the hints of heaven in this fallen place; it celebrates the relentless foretastes of hell that are strewn all about us. Hell will be many things, but one thing it will be is the absence of beauty. There will be nothing to lift a man above the ugliness that litters hell. I don't doubt that the ship may sound and look like hell, but your job, Stuart, is to flood that floating Hades with the light of truth, beauty, and the love of Christ. Press on, Sailor!"

Art as Imitation

Everyone wants to be original—especially artists. But herein lies the problem and the great challenge. All art is imitative. Art is not the real thing; it is the artificial thing. So art that imitates dark and sinful things in nonredemptive ways is imitating the wrong things. Like the "art" preferred by sailors on Stuart's ship, that art will inevitably be an ugly imitation of hell.

It all starts with theology. Only in a world severed from moral absolutes can art be anything the artist wants it to be. Not so in the real world. In our world an artist can bag up his own excrement, dub it "art," and send it to museums to be displayed at the expense of the grossed-out but dutifully unprotesting public. In God's world—the real world—this is nonredemptive and ugly, and therefore not art.

It is perhaps not surprising that man's theological rebellion against God, the ultimate original Creator of all beauty, finds virulent expression in art. Many artists are affronted that they cannot be ultimate originators of anything. Desperate to assert their authority over creative expression, they are driven to innovate. They don't want to be seen as imitators of anything or anyone—especially not the Creator God of the Bible. Thus, in a world devoid of absolute values, the value of art is measured by individual expression, innovation, and the bizarre. And artists continue to insist that their "art represents the source of human values."

Play by the intellectual elitists' rules, and you will no longer be able to define beauty or art. Accept the cultural elitists' supposed authority over art, and that authority will encompass every other area of life. It's what they want. Remember how expansively they speak about art: "Art gives meaning to life." Accept their authority over art, and eventually things such as truth, liberty, and justice will also be defined by the elite. Tyranny in art leads to tyranny in everything else.

When political leaders see themselves as "the makers of manners," as Shakespeare's Henry V quipped to his battle-prize bride, law and justice are redefined for the self-gratification of the tyrant. So in matters of art. The elite are not the makers of artistic manners, though they work very hard at intimidating us into believing this. Art, like truth and justice, must be guided by universal absolutes; otherwise, we live in an inconsistent world, a world none of us can count on, a world without gravity, a chaotic and ugly world.

Socrates, on a quest for the source of wisdom, discovered that Greek artisans, though skillful with stone, were unwise because they projected their skill with the chisel into the notion "that they also knew all sorts of high matters." Socrates concluded his inquiry with the words, "God only is wise"—or, put another way: Man's skill, his wisdom, in any field is the gift of God, the great Originator of all skill.

A wise ancient poet put it still better. "The fear of the LORD is the beginning of wisdom, and knowledge of the Holy One is understanding" (Prov. 9:10). Do you want skill (wisdom) to appreciate or create beautiful art? Fear the Lord; he alone is the "beginning of wisdom."

A wise man, then, acknowledges that his skill is not innate but derived, given to him from above, a gift of God, regulated by his laws. So throughout the Bible, art is a means of reflecting the glory of God, the Originator of all creative beauty. However unsophisticated it sounds to the world's ears, God, *de jure*, by right, defines both beauty and art.

Gaze on Ultimate Beauty

Perhaps the advice biblically informed Shakespeare has Hamlet give actors helps shed light on these questions about art. The Bard wrote that the purpose of his art was "to hold the mirror up to nature, to show virtue her own features." Shakespeare's summary of the imitative purpose of art sounds odd in a world that is morally, intellectually, spiritually, and aesthetically adrift. When the world rejects absolutes, it loses the capability of showing "virtue her own features" in art, or in any other dimension of life.

Though it is possible for an artist to create a worthy image of something that is not beautiful at first blush (crucifixion is not beautiful), all artistic endeavor must be regulated by the light of God's Word. Paul in his letter to the Philippians gives us the final word about art and life: "Finally, brothers, whatever is true, whatever is noble, whatever is right, whatever is pure, whatever is lovely, whatever is admirable—if anything is excellent or praiseworthy—think about such things" (Phil. 4:8).

Therefore, the Christian young man will set before his mind and eyes only art that leads to truth, purity, and loveliness. Art worthy of the title must be excellent and praiseworthy. But not according to the transient opinions of elitist critics—excellent and praiseworthy according to God's definition. And know this: in the Bible, *excellent* and *praiseworthy* are not subjective terms.

Vast and wonderfully varied as human creativity and art is, a subject worthy of a lifetime of enjoyment and discovery, how does a young man keep his way pure in matters of art? Be like the psalmist: "One thing I ask of the LORD, this is what I seek: that I may dwell in the house of the LORD all the days of my life, to gaze upon the beauty of the LORD . . ." Live your life gazing on the beauty of the Lord, and you will have little difficulty defining beauty, appreciating beauty, or creating beauty.

Prayer Resolves

- To cultivate discernment in art not from artists but from God's Word
- To set no unworthy thing before my eyes
- Varied as art is, to think about two paths in art: one that leads to heaven and the other to hell

Scripture Memory

"Finally, brothers, whatever is true, whatever is noble, whatever is right, whatever is pure, whatever is lovely, whatever is admirable—if anything is excellent or praiseworthy—think about such things."

Philippians 4:8

For Discussion

1. When and how should sinful things be the subject matter of art?

2. Some art depicts sinful things in redemptive ways; some art does not. With your dad, look through an art-history book, identifying redemptive elements.
3. Discuss nudity in art. Is it the same as pornography? Why or why not? Discuss the role of the viewer in appreciating art.

"Rise, My Soul, to Watch and Pray"

Watch! Let not the wicked world with its power defeat thee.
Watch lest with her pomp unfurled she betray and cheat thee.
Watch and see lest there be faithless friends to charm thee,
Who but seek to harm thee.

Johann Freystein, 1697

For Further Study

Exodus 31:1–11; 35:30–39:31; 1 Kings 5–6; *Art for God's Sake*, by Philip Graham Ryken

12

THE DEAD WHITE MALES

Daniel 1:17; Acts 17:28; Numbers 21:27

I read a tragic axiom the other day: "If you want to keep a secret from an African, put it in a book." The telling expression is used by Ugandan teachers who lament their students' lack of interest in books. Though most Ugandans can read at some level, few read for recreation or for information. They're not to be faulted for this. Books are expensive. The average Ugandan makes a mere $280 per year. For the sake of comparison, $280 is what a lawyer friend of mine earns in one hour. And reading takes time. In most of Africa, time is already committed to eking out a living.

We have nothing like their excuse. But I wonder how long before it will be said, "If you want to keep a secret from an American, put it in a book." In a recent Zogby poll, 60 percent of Americans identified Homer as Bart Simpson's father; a mere 21 percent knew Homer as the ancient Greek poet and could name one of his epics. The other 19 percent? I shudder to think.

In *The Voyage of the Dawn Treader*, C. S. Lewis identifies one of the root problems for one of his most insufferable characters: "Eustace had read none of the right books." He elaborates: "Eustace had read only the wrong books. They had a lot to say about exports and imports and governments and drains, but they were weak on dragons."

Lewis loved stories about heroism, knights, brave deeds against the odds, the triumph of good over evil—and about talking animals. But the right books for Lewis weren't just for entertainment or diversion. He believed that books make the man. Far more than providing fodder for small talk at parties, the right books can profoundly change those who read them. It's what makes them the right books.

Young men today are growing up in a culture at war with the right books. A recent National Endowment for the Arts report called "Reading at Risk" found a drastic decline in reading classic literature among all Americans but especially among young adults. That is tragic. Most theorists connect this plummet in reading books to the rise of popular culture, conveyed through TV (think *The Simpsons*), DVDs, computer games, and music.

Clearly, this is not the way God intended a culture to organize itself. He revealed himself to man in a Book, one he intended us to read. Hence, the ultimate goal of all reading ought to be to know and obey God as he has revealed himself in his Book—the Word.

Death to Old Books

Postmodern literary criticism, however, has decreed an entirely new way of reading books. When you read old books—if you must—you read to expose the racism and sexism of the dead, white, and predominantly male authors. You read to expose all their prejudices and unenlightened assumptions. Read books any other way and you lack sophistication, even basic intelligence, and you will probably have a difficult time passing your English classes.

No single factor is more responsible for the war on old books today than what Lewis called "chronological snobbery," the unexamined assumption that we are the enlightened ones, that today we know better than those who came before us. In short, every generation is inclined to look back at the past and snort in derision at how barbaric those ignorant roughs were, and then to dub their age the "Dark Ages."

This chronological snobbery ensures the self-referentialism that ultimately cuts off men from an essential source of wisdom. "The failure to read good books," wrote cultural critic Allan Bloom, "both enfeebles the vision and strengthens our most fatal tendency—the belief that the here and now is all there is." Thus, Lewis urges us to "keep the clean sea breezes of the centuries blowing through our minds." And this "can be done only by reading old books."

Elitist crafters of culture, decrying the dead-white-male patriarchy of the old books, are certain that no enlightened thinking person would impose Shakespeare and Spenser, or Austen and O'Connor, on students. In our multicultural world, they say, these authors have nothing to say to today's diverse population. Gleefully, the elitists expose the authors' perceived folly, rather than humbly allowing the authors to expose theirs. These elitists have become, as Lewis has it, critics where they ought to be pupils. In his classic *Screwtape Letters*, Lewis explains how it works:

> In the intellectual climate which we [Screwtape and the demons] have at last succeeded in producing . . . only the learned read old books, and we have now so dealt with the learned that they are of all men the least likely to acquire wisdom by doing so. When a learned man is presented with any statement in an ancient author, the one question he never asks is whether it is true. He asks who influenced the ancient writer, and how far the statement is consistent with what he said in other books, and what phase in the writer's development, or in the general history of thought, it illustrates and how it affected later writers, and how often it has been misunderstood (especially by the learned man's own colleagues) and what the general course of criticism on it has been for the last ten years, and what is the "present state of the question." To regard the ancient writer as a possible source of knowledge—to anticipate that what he said could possibly modify your thoughts or your behavior—this would be rejected as unutterably simple-minded. And since we cannot deceive the whole

> human race all the time, it is most important thus to cut every generation off from all others; for where learning makes a free commerce between the ages there is always the danger that the characteristic errors of one may be corrected by the characteristic truths of another.

Perceptively, Lewis unmasks the thinly veiled conspiracy to silence the wisdom and worldview of the past embodied in the canon of Western literature. Today's educators don't want students to read these authors because they don't want the next generation to think the way the wisest minds and imaginations have thought.

Postmodern cultural gurus are determined to "cut every generation off from all others" because they do not want students to believe, as the authors of the great books believed, that there is "a divinity that shapes our ends" (Shakespeare's *Hamlet*), that "all actions must beware of the powers beyond us" (Sophocles' *Oedipus the King*), that "in the course of justice none of us should see salvation; we do pray for mercy, and that same prayer doth teach us to render the deeds of mercy" (Shakespeare's *Merchant of Venice*), that "man desires to be more than man to rule his world for himself" (Sophocles' *Oedipus the King*).

The new crafters of culture desperately do not want students to read authors who believe that men are subject to transcendent authority, that morality is informed by absolute truth, and that actions have objective consequences in a real world. Yet every worthy author in the Western canon believed in these things, the very ideas that postmodern educators are dumping from the curriculum.

Flannery O'Connor, who wrote new books, understood how central old books were to the curriculum: "It is a good rule, after reading a new book, never to allow yourself another new one till you have read an old one in between." After arguing that students must read old books in school, she concluded, "And if the student finds that this is not to his taste? Well, that is regrettable. Most regrettable. His taste should not be consulted; it is being formed."

"As Literature"

I was mystified by an assignment that my daughter was given in a college English course. Students were to write a comparison of the writing style of several authors. They were specifically instructed not to compare the content, just the stylistic medium employed. I was reminded of the Imagist poet Archibald MacLeish: "a poem should not mean / But be."

Apparently my daughter's English professor believed that the style of the author was more important than the accuracy with which he represented reality and the nature of things. Augustine used to read books this way, until by the grace of God he underwent a radical change, a change that affected his appreciation of literature. He finally came to understand that "not the manner but the matter of a discourse is to be cared for."

Some public schools allow students to study the Bible if they study it only as literature, an approach that Joel Belz describes as "terribly shackled." The phrase "as literature" further mystifies me. What does it mean? Do we read John Milton to gush over the way he uses subordinate clauses? Or do we read with the view of coming to absurd little conclusions such as this: "I love what Daniel Defoe does with semicolons"?

To read anything "as literature" is just another way to avoid at all costs asking whether what the author wrote is true. Still more to be avoided is changing one's behavior if what he wrote is true. Instead, we'll just look at how clever he is with words and figures of speech. End of analysis—but never "regard the ancient writer as a possible source of knowledge." Go ahead and read Shakespeare and the Bible, if you must, but don't read with any notion of having your thoughts or behavior radically modified by what you read.

Censorship

Comic Dave Barry once wrote in a column on kids and homework, "I have never been a big fan of *Beowulf* or epic poems in general:

'Epic,' in my opinion, is a code word that English teachers use for 'boring,' the same way they use 'satirical' when they mean 'you will not laugh once.' "

Barry's not alone. Since 1987, when Jesse Jackson led a protest march at Stanford University at which students chanted, "Hey, hey, ho, ho, Western culture's got to go," the study of literature on American campuses has undergone drastic renovation. Today more than 70 percent of college English majors are never required to take a single course in Beowulf or Shakespeare or any other form of Western classical literature.

While I was attending a seminar at a local college, an English professor handed me several pages of guidelines for teaching college preparatory English. Dave Barry's worst nightmare: forty high school English teachers discussing why so few high school graduates can write decent essays. I glanced over the guidelines.

"Students must read multicultural texts," read the first guideline, the foundation on which the entire writing curriculum was built. The problem started making sense. In the state of Washington where I teach English, sophomores must take an exam and actually show mastery of essay-writing. But we're in crisis. Appallingly few sophomores can pass the exam.

"Why can't these kids write essays?" teachers moan. "They can't even form a thesis statement."

I attempted to offer an explanation. "Students can't write essays because essays are built around logical evidence that proves what is true about a topic. Our educational philosophy teaches kids that there are no moral absolutes. If there are no absolute truths, then what ought to surprise us is that anyone ever came up with the idea of writing essays in the first place. Why bother writing about what a historical event or a book means if nothing means anything?"

Finally, it goes back to the starting guideline: "Students must read multicultural texts." Cut students off from the great writers down through the centuries, and we forfeit the right to be astonished that

they can't write. They've been forbidden to feast on the timeless, enduring models of great writing. Of course they can't write.

Right Book—Wrong Book

Here's how illogical this all becomes. Barry Lynn, director of Americans United for the Separation of Church and State, termed Lewis's *The
Lion, the Witch and the Wardrobe* "totally inappropriate" for American
public schools. "It is simply a retelling of the story of Christ."

Ironically, a week earlier during Banned Books Week, this same
Barry Lynn had attacked Christians from Alabama who had chosen not
to use certain textbooks in their Christian school because of anti-Christian bias in the books. Absurdly, he cried "censorship" when Christians made a curriculum decision for a privately funded school, but a
week later felt justified in calling for a ban on Lewis's books in public
schools. To this kind of convoluted reasoning, Lewis would probably
say, "Logic! Why don't they teach logic at these schools?"

Not only do they attempt to oppose great books on legal and
constitutional grounds, anti-Christian elites attempt to marginalize the
literary quality of books that contain Christian themes.

Those who shape arguments win them. One of the pet ways in
which the literary elite shape this argument is to insist that books are
better when they're just rip-roaring good yarns. Literary elites think it's
great if a book uses Eastern mysticism, or if it's sexual or scatological,
or if it's informed by moral relativism or naturalism. But when readers
point out how great authors employ Christian allegory and celebrate
Christian morality and themes, crafters of culture snort in derision.

If they were honest, postmodernists would admit that they find
the "manner" of a book more to their liking when the "matter" fits their
worldview assumptions. Allow me to illustrate.

In 1995, *My Own Sweet Time* was published as a memoir ostensibly
written by an Aboriginal black female named Wanda Koolmatrie. The
book was hailed as a triumph by feminists and multiculturalists, and
cash literary awards and fat royalty checks started pouring into Wanda's

lap. Then word got out. "Wanda" was a forty-seven-year-old white male taxi driver who had worn himself out trying to get his writing published. Leon Carmen finally figured things out. If you were a fat white male, publishers weren't much interested in what you wrote (poor Winston Churchill), but if you wrote as a black female, the world gushed.

The media largely buried the story because the implications to feminism and multiculturalism were too revealing, but this egg-on-face episode in publishing underscores the enormous fallacy of using gender and racial criteria for determining whether a book is the right book or not.

Divine Plot

Postmodern literary criteria work poorly at best, but they especially malfunction in retrospect. If literature is more magnificent when Christian truth and morality are absent and feminist, multicultural agendas are front and center, someone forgot to tell a great many authors down through the centuries.

Clearly, John Milton failed to fall in line when he penned *Paradise Lost*, the great English epic based on the biblical account of the fall of man. Milton makes no apologies for his epic being an argument for obedience to God and to "justify the ways of God to man."

Or read Edmund Spenser's *Faerie Queene*, or Dante's *Divine Comedy*, or John Bunyan's *Pilgrim's Progress* and *Holy War*, to name but a few. These universally accepted literary masterpieces, like many of their counterparts in music and visual art, are unashamedly biblical and Christian. These authors and many others, including Shakespeare, clearly did not believe that literary art is less majestic when it is informed by biblical truth and morality. Neither did Lewis, who believed that "all history is a story with a divine plot."

Frankly, it's absurd to think that Western literature would be as majestic without Christ figures and biblical images. Every author who has ever put pen to paper, Christian or otherwise, is made in God's image. It would be odd indeed if literature written by divine image-bearers *didn't* employ divine imagery!

Read for Wisdom

There are many demands on a young man's time: family, church, school, and sports (and then there's video games, movies, music, and the like). So why reorganize the limited time that you have around reading old books? What could they possibly contain that would be worth it?

In his book *An Experiment in Criticism*, C. S. Lewis offered one of the best answers to why reading old books is so important: "The nearest I have yet got to an answer is that we seek an enlargement of our being. We want to see with other eyes, to imagine with other imaginations, to feel with other hearts, as well as with our own. In coming to understand anything we are rejecting the facts as they are for us in favor of the facts as they are." Young men have many flawed assumptions about themselves and the world. Old books can help expose those errors, and strengthen your arm to annihilate them.

A wealth of riches lie within the pages of the great books, riches that young men—if they are to become strong men, even heroes—must read and reread. Precisely because you are young and inexperienced, you must read and pass through the vicarious experiences available in classic literature. Many of those books were written by Christians, but just as many were written by unbelievers, pagans such as Homer (not Bart's dad), Sophocles, and Cicero.

As a young man Augustine, born and raised in Africa, read one of Cicero's great classics, *Hortensius*. Of this unbeliever's writing Augustine wrote, "This book altered my affections and made me address prayers to thee, O Lord, giving me other desires and purposes than I had before. Cicero . . . stirred up and kindled and inflamed me . . . to loving, and seeking, and finding, and holding, and inseparably embracing of Wisdom itself, wheresoever it might be."

This is how a young man knows whether he's reading the right books. If those books stir up, kindle, and inflame in you the deepest desire to know true wisdom, then you can be sure you're reading the right books.

May it never be said that if you want to keep a secret from an American young man, put it in a book. Read the right books, but always read first and last, and hold in the highest esteem, the greatest of all old books—the Bible.

Prayer Resolves

- To temper my love of play by cultivating a love of reading
- To evaluate every book by the best of books, the Bible

Scripture Memory

"To these four young men God gave knowledge and understanding of all kinds of literature and learning."

Daniel 1:17

For Discussion

1. Compare and contrast books and reading with TV, movies, video games, and so on.
2. Do you become a better TV-watcher in any similar way to becoming a better reader? If not, why not?
3. Discuss the benefits and dangers of reading literature written by non-Christian authors.

"Shepherd of Tender Youth"

Forever be our Guide,
Our Shepherd and our pride,
Our staff and song;
Jesus, O Christ of God,
By your perennial Word,
Lead us where you have trod;
Make our faith strong.

Clement of Alexandria, ca. 200

For Further Study

Consider starting a father-and-son reading club in which you read classic books; Numbers 21:27; Acts 17:28

YOUNG MEN: CULTURE, HUMANITY, TRUTH, AND LIES

13

CULTURE DECONSTRUCTED

John 14:6

Death to Education

"There are no wrong answers," intoned Dr. Jones. I remember trying to process these words as I sat in a graduate class at a Benedictine university. Professor Jones continued: "In order for students to feel free to express their opinions in class, 'Instruction must embrace and affirm all the beliefs, values, and traditions of the diversity of students in the classroom.' " It was an obligatory mantra, straight from the education textbooks. I'd heard it before. She paused, looking around the room for a response.

Part of me wanted to laugh, but the nonsensical theory dominating educational philosophy today is no laughing matter. Rapidly a plan formed in my mind.

"That's ridiculous," I said, as respectfully as one can say those words. The room fell silent. Dr. Jones blinked and stared back at me.

"With respect, Dr. Jones, I'm simply trying to move your instruction from theory to application. I'm a student. You're the teacher. Is my response as a student a right or a wrong answer?"

She made no reply. I felt sorry for her; nevertheless, I pressed my point. "Can you explain to me how you can embrace and affirm my response to what you have just taught us? You have taught us that there are no wrong answers. Again, I ask, is my answer, then, a correct one or an incorrect one?"

To Dr. Jones's credit, she nodded her head and mumbled something about the message being received. But by precious few in the educational establishment.

Right or Wrong?

After sweating bullets for two and a half hours, I completed an essay examination answering the question: "Should multiculturalism shape the curriculum?" Essentially, I argued that if multiculturalism shaped the school curriculum, education by any meaningful definition would be over.

The next day, the dean of the education department at the university called me at school. The secretary tried to explain that I was teaching a class. The dean was insistent. She prefaced her comments with some form of the "there-are-no-wrong-answers" mantra. Then she proceeded to say that she found my essay offensive to diversity, insensitive, intolerant, and racist. I listened to her rant, and when she paused for breath I attempted to reply.

I reiterated that if multiculturalism consistently shaped the school curriculum, we would lose all ability to grade anything. There would no longer be any evaluative perspective from which to measure student achievement. If every cultural idea were as valid as any other, teachers would be reduced to offering anemic surveys of equally valid ideas. No conclusions could be drawn about anything. If there really were no wrong or right answers, then why bother teaching or learning anything?

She disagreed. I tried to help the dean see that her disagreement was proof positive that at the gut level she did agree with the basic premise of my essay: that all conclusions are not equal, that some answers are right and some are wrong. The fact that she believed my conclusions were wrong, like it or not, proves that they're right. Things got a bit icy on the other end of the line.

At some point even those who profess to be the most tolerant can't tolerate something or someone, and it's invariably Christians whom they cannot tolerate. Ironically, those who say that there are no wrong answers are often the first to decry how wrong Christianity is. There is something fundamentally flawed, however, when a worldview shoots itself in the intellectual foot like this. How valid is a philosophy that claims that tolerance is the highest good, while being intolerant of all who disagree?

Did Not Fit Our Beliefs

After a kayak-team barbecue where I was asked to pray by the host family, I received an e-mail that illustrates the faulty logic of multiculturalism. The subject of the e-mail was labeled "Diversity." It began like this:

"This is a difficult letter to write as it addresses a sensitive issue, but I feel very strongly that I need to speak my mind.

"I think that giving thanks to G-d before a meal is a fine tradition. I support your effort last night at the kayak team party in bringing people together and in making what could be a chaotic grab for food a more refined moment of counting our blessings. However, some of us have different beliefs and I was disheartened that you didn't take that into account in your prayer.

"My son and I are Jewish. Maybe there are others in our group that are of different faiths. A prayer to G-d feels fine. Most people of the world have a belief in a G-d. But we all don't believe that Jesus is our G-d. To present a prayer for the whole group in the name of Jesus did not fit our beliefs and made my son and me and perhaps some others uncomfortable, so that the whole intent of your moment of worship didn't sit well and made us feel peripheral to your prayer. It set us apart rather than gathering us into a circle of friendship. We were not at your church or at a celebration of a Christian holiday, but at a kayak team event. We are a diverse group and as such we need to respect this in each other . . ."

In Jesus' Name

I prayed as I offered my reply to this secular Jewess with French heritage.

"I'm so glad that you wrote to me about this! I really do appreciate you doing so and the spirit in which you did it. I want to assure you that my reason for praying in Jesus' name was not thoughtlessly to offend you or your son, or others who might be of other religions than Christianity or who might, in fact, be atheists.

"The subject of your e-mail was 'Diversity.' True diversity, it seems to me, celebrates and allows diversity in others. Our hosts are Christians, as we are, and they pray in Jesus' name whether they have guests in their home or not, as we do in ours. Our Christian hosts asked me to pray before the meal. I'm confident that if you hosted the kayak club in your home, and prayed before the meal, you would pray according to your beliefs.

"And if an atheist on the team hosted the club and chose not to pray at all, that, too, would reflect true diversity. I would not be offended if atheists did not pray, nor would I expect atheists to look around their dining room and feel obligated to offer some kind of prayer that would appease all present (an impossible task).

"The absence of prayer for atheists accurately expresses their beliefs about God. And when a Christian prays in Jesus' name, he, too, is accurately expressing his beliefs. But expecting everyone to reduce their religious practices to the lowest common denominator of all present seems to me precisely to represent not diversity but instead an anemic, monochromatic uniformity required of all. By definition, diversity means that there will be differences.

"Now, if I had required everyone to repeat after me, or to join in a corporate Amen or go hungry, that would have violated diversity. But praying as I have been taught, as I have always prayed, as I believe it is right to pray, but not requiring anyone to either agree or disagree with me—you may disagree with that prayer, but it certainly cannot be a violation of true diversity.

"If I were at your home and insisted on praying aloud in Jesus' name, that would be a violation. It seems to me that if I were at your home and expected you to pray in a way that fit with my understanding of praying, that would not be allowing you to be diverse from me. Isn't that what diversity actually is? Allowing Jews to be Jews, and atheists to be atheists, and Christians to be Christians—that's diversity. Our hosts are Christians. So am I. We pray to God in Jesus' name. That's what devout Christians have always done.

"The reason? Christ is everything to Christians. To a Jew or another non-trinitarian monotheist, praying to 'God' is an accurate expression of their belief. For a Christian, however, to omit Christ in his praying is not an accurate expression of his beliefs. It's not who we are and does not reflect what we believe.

"It seems to me that people who place a high priority on diversity would go out of their way to try and not change the practices of someone who believes differently than they do.

"Finally, Christianity is not about tradition, or taste; it's about truth. I pray in the name of Jesus Christ (a Jew) because he is God. I don't pray with a view to pleasing or displeasing other people (though I certainly am not intentionally trying to offend people as I do).

"I don't think devout people of any faith pray to please others. A Muslim doesn't pray to please people; he prays to please Allah. I pray to God and, according to the light I have been given, to Jesus Christ as God and Savior. How can I do otherwise? I am a sinner under God's just wrath for breaking his holy law. God has mercifully pitched his love on me, unworthy as I am. He did so by sending his precious Son, the Anointed One, Jesus Christ, to bear the penalty of my sins, to pay the debt I could not pay, to die in my place on a Roman gibbet, to rise from the dead, and to ascend to the Father, there to make intercession for me. Now when God looks at my unworthy life, he sees the perfect righteousness of Jesus Christ, who suffered and died in my place. There is nothing more wonderful in all the world, and I love the Lord Jesus very much as a result. How can I profane him by bowing to cultural pressure to not name him whenever and wherever I am? To do so is spiritual treason for Christians.

"My Christian forebears died in Roman amphitheaters, and a host of my spiritual relatives have given their lives throughout the ages, and many do so today (Sudan, China, Indonesia, Saudi Arabia . . .). Why? For naming Christ alone as God and as their Savior and Lord. I love Christ. I love being a Christian. It is my calling and my holy obligation to share Jesus' name with everyone.

"I am sorry if I offended you by naming Jesus in my prayer. But it seems to me that my offense can't have been against diversity. As the French say, *Viva la difference*! That's diversity . . ."

Diversity Unmasked

At the end of the day, none of this has anything to do with diversity and tolerance. The woman I corresponded with on diversity let it slip when she said that my prayer "did not fit [her] beliefs." So diversity somehow obligates me to pray in a way that fits her beliefs? A few gurus of multiculturalism and diversity have also let their real agenda get out.

While academia and political correctness demand tolerance of everything from gay marriage to infanticide, Richard Dawkins insists that "religious myths ought not to be tolerated." Dawkins, an Oxford professor, called by an orthodox Jewish rabbi "one of the generals in the anti-Christian army of the secular left," goes so far as to suggest that the secular state has a right and obligation to protect children from parents' religious beliefs. "It's one thing to say people should be free to believe whatever they like, but should they be free to impose their beliefs on their children?" At least he's honest; Dawkins candidly admits that his tolerance does not extend to Christians. Nor does he want to see diversity in science instruction. He insists that evolutionary naturalism be the only voice, not a particularly tolerant and diverse demand.

Dawkins wants the knife to cut only one way. If children should be protected from their parents' beliefs, why only children of Christians? Why not children of naturalists, too? Because multicultural crafters of culture believe that their ideas are right and Christian ones are wrong, all while claiming that there are no wrong answers.

Bill Watterson hints at all this in one of his comics. Calvin is squirming away in his desk during a math test. "2+7= _____" has Calvin stumped. After fidgeting some more, Calvin scrawls on his paper, "I cannot answer this question, as it is against my religious principles." Watterson may be suggesting that in the illogical world the multiculturalists are attempting to fabricate, offering students only one blank for their answer is to suggest the inherently religious idea that there is, lo and behold, only one right answer.

I'm reminded of what C. S. Lewis writes in *God in the Dock*. He points out that those who believe Christianity to be true and those who do not will both "be very keen about education: but the kinds of education they wanted people to have would obviously be very different." Education is inherently religious, but educational elites refuse to acknowledge that their Darwinian evolutionary view of the world is not neutral; it's based on a religious belief called *naturalism*.

Multiculturalism is a power grab that depends on the radical redefining of words. It's what happens when people with a subversive agenda shape the argument. Call it *multiculturalism*, and you're free to silence the ideas of any who disagree with you. This rhetorical back door to tyranny goes like this: "We'll tolerate everyone—except anyone who doesn't toe the line on our ideas about tolerance. Deviate from our diversity dogma, and you'll find us the most intolerant of folks. Pray, if you must, but make sure you do it so it fits with our beliefs." This is absurdity—not diversity. But it sure works well at silencing those whose views you hate.

Finally, multiculturalism is intolerant of Christians because our belief is exclusive—there is no other God and Savior. Jesus Christ declared himself to be "the way and the truth and the life. No one comes to the Father except through me" (John 14:6). That is Christian belief, and it is absolutely exclusive; hence, multiculturalism was crafted precisely to silence that exclusivity. It may prove to be a setup for religious persecution.

Multi-Absurdism

Diversity *ad absurdum* spirals into banning pigs in parts of once-great Britain so as not to offend an increasingly militant Muslim population. So it's no more Winnie the Pooh and Piglet. Folks in Britain are now intolerant of A. A. Milne because he is insensitive to Muslims who are offended by pigs. Every edict of toleration has a backlash of intolerance for someone.

But it gets worse. Now many British schools "avoid teaching the Holocaust . . . because they do not want to cause offense" to the growing Muslim population, reported the BBC. After all, many Muslims the world over would have agreed with Nazi extermination of Jews in the Holocaust. "Israel must be wiped off the map," Iranian President Mahmoud Ahmadinejad said in a recent speech. Apparently British educational elites have chosen to tolerate Muslims—but not Jews.

Contrarily, José Aznar, the former prime minister of Spain, delivered an address in which he offered a more clear-sighted solution to the diversity disaster: "We must recover our principles, the deepest roots of Europe—for example, our Christian roots, our own cultural beliefs, setting aside the enormous error of multiculturalism. The multicultural experiment has failed." He argued that redefining tolerance has diverted many from "the true expression of tolerance: equality under the law." Europe has lost its moral compass because "we refuse to call things by their proper names." He concluded that the corrective to failed multiculturalism starts with the understanding that "we are engaged in a battle of civilizations."

True Diversity

While the jargon of diversity is employed as a club to silence Christianity, ironically, it's in the Christian church that true diversity exists. Christ's reign enfolds three hundred million people in Africa, an innumerable host in China, India, South America, and beyond to a host that no man can number. John wrote of Christ, "You are worthy to take the scroll and to open its seals, because you were slain, and with your blood you purchased men for God from every tribe and language and people and nation" (Rev. 5:9).

Reformer John Calvin understood this true diversity. The church "is not one state, not one people, but as far and as wide as the earth extends; it has obtained its authority by the holy concord of divers peoples, who otherwise disagreeing in everything among themselves, ought to move us greatly, since it is clear that this agreement is brought about by nothing else than the divine will."

This is true diversity. Certainly, in our churches we must more faithfully extend the love of Christ to our neighbors regardless of race or socioeconomic status. Nevertheless, nowhere is "the holy concord of divers peoples" more obvious than in the church of Jesus Christ throughout the centuries, and throughout the world.

God's sovereign purpose has always been to create, out of a multi-ethnic panoply of language, race, and national identity, one gathered-in, monocultural people, one vast, elect nation. Hence, Christian men are duty bound to strive, by loving proclamation of the truth, for one culture, one cult, one belief extended to all. That is true diversity. O Lord, hasten the day!

Prayer Resolves

- To understand the strategies of multiculturalism to silence Christians
- To love my neighbor regardless of race

Scripture Memory

"You are worthy to take the scroll and to open its seals, because you were slain, and with your blood you purchased men for God from every tribe and language and people and nation."

Revelation 5:9

For Discussion

1. How do multiculturalists shape the discussion so that truth and ideas are confused with race and gender?
2. How can you be prepared to expose this fallacy? Practice doing so by role-playing.

"Shout, for the Blessed Jesus Reigns"

Gentiles and Jews his laws obey;
Nations remote their offering bring,
And unconstrained their homage pay
To their exalted God and King.

Benjamin Beddome, 1769

For Further Study

Psalm 22:27–30; John 12:32

14

MALE AND FEMALE DECONSTRUCTED

1 Peter 3:7

Throw Off the Shackles

In a former life, while working as a commercial photojournalist, I was sent on an assignment to do a photo session with a log-truck driver—a woman. My corporate client thought it would make a great story. I was expecting a tattooed male wannabe in cork boots and Carhartts with a pinch of Copenhagen in her cheek.

What I found was a weary single mom who had taken the job driving a log truck because she needed work. She'd done her hair for the photo shoot, and her work shirt was neatly pressed. I actually caught one of the best grab shots of my career when she glanced at her reflection in her driver's-side mirror and whipped out her lipstick for a quick primp. Rather than a freak show, I encountered a pitiful casualty of feminism.

Feminism has been around since the fall. To the woman God said, "Your desire will be for your husband, and he will rule over you" (Gen. 3:16b), that is to say, she will want to rule over him, but in the end, men will dominate women. This is not an imperative; it's a straightforward statement of fact. It's just what is.

The latest wave of women attempting to usurp the headship that God ordained for men has been with us for about a generation. Simone de Beauvoir's book *The Second Sex* (1949) was a potent argument for equality by sameness. Men and women are not different from each other by nature, de Beauvoir insisted, but by socialization. Men have oppressed women and have treated them as the second sex, and women are tired of being subordinate to men. She maintained that women could be just as aggressive and assertive as men and that they needed to free themselves from dependence on men. Her book established the theory that encouraged women to "throw off the shackles of yesterday" by imitating men.

Then along came Betty Friedan's book *The Feminine Mystique* (1963). Friedan furthered the attack against femininity by arguing that women have been oppressed by being forced to be feminine. Men, she claimed, admire women for their feminine beauty, but only as means of enslaving them as wives and mothers, who then live out their miserable existences raising children and doing housework.

Shameless Sameness

How to fix this oppressive system? "We need to raise boys like we raise girls," Gloria Steinem insists, apparently assuming that girl behavior is normal and boy behavior is abnormal. Fueled by militant feminists, this educational philosophy was gobbled up by educators, especially university professors, spawning whole new departments, forever changing the character of higher education.

I had a professor with a Ph.D. in women's studies who was known for bullying graduate students into research topics that exposed the sexism of patriarchy. He frequently launched into tirades against male-dominated society. "All gender differences are purely the result of socialization," he would say, as if anyone who thought otherwise had two left arms.

After one such tirade, a woman in her thirties raised her hand and asked whether he had children. He wasn't sure what that had to do with anything, but admitted he hadn't. "If you were raising a son and a daughter, as I am," she said, "you would never say things like that. Boys and girls are just plain different."

My wife and I heard a similar statement from a hand-wringing liberal midwife. "If anyone raised her children to be gender-neutral," she said, "it was me." Bewildered, she went on to describe how her little girl unaccountably loved pink and frills, and how her boy turned dollies into trucks and plowed them through the dirt. She didn't like the fact, but she was, nevertheless, honest enough to admit it.

George Gilder, senior fellow at the Discovery Institute, described the effect that this assumption has had on university education. "Most of these institutions have flounced through the last forty years fashioning a fluffy pink playpen of feminist studies and 'herstory.' " Little wonder that "men now receive only 41 percent of new bachelors' degrees." Gilder then cites a reality that he says "may prompt the tenured ladies at Harvard and MIT to burst into tears and summon lawyers to sue God: the absence of boys in colleges does not mean that women suddenly began writing most of our leading-edge software programs or designing microchips for our missile defenses."

In other words, feminists can protest in the streets and write their books—but none of that changes the nature of things. You can't defeat reality; though a woman's desire will be to take over the man's role, men will, in the end, rule over her (Gen. 3:16b).

Unnecessary Mistakes

Bible-believing Christians have always understood that "God created man in his own image . . . ; male and female he created them" (Gen. 1:27). Thus, the difference between men and women is in the nature of creation, and God has ordained that difference for the good of both men and women. Christians have also understood that big trouble awaits those who defy God's design for men and women.

Increasingly, however, cultural critics without a declared Christian commitment are observing that feminism is leading to profound cultural problems. Several have been brave enough to publish their conclusions.

"Feminism, in its eagerness to claim manliness for women," writes Harvard professor Harvey C. Mansfield, "destroyed femininity." He cites the Herculean efforts of Hollywood moviemakers to reverse gender roles by making women dominant characters in war movies, pirate movies, and gangster films. Fueled by de Beauvoir and Friedan, women have scrambled to prove that whatever men can do, women can do better by liberating themselves from husbands and children, by seeking male jobs, and by climbing the corporate ladder. "We can be just like men" became the cry of women.

Mansfield argues that in all this, feminism has tried to deny the "basic truth" about men and women: they're different by nature. Thus, militant feminists' imposing gender-neutrality on society "sounds like liberation," he wrote, "but it isn't." Society needs "to make it honorable again that a woman be a woman, and a man a man."

Most women have an intuitive sense of the essential differences between the sexes, but, Mansfield says, "feminism does not allow them to think about it. You can say that men and women are not different, but if you try to live your life by that belief you will make many unnecessary mistakes." In order to avoid those "mistakes," he recommends that feminism's insistence on the sameness of men and women "be abandoned as contrary to common sense."

Dr. Mansfield, be it known, is far from the only secularist speaking out against the failure of feminism. But Dr. Mansfield is a man. What does he know about women?

Women against Feminism

One nearly universal observation made about modern liberated women is how profoundly unhappy and anxious about their lives they are. Caitlin Flanagan, staff writer for *The New Yorker*, explains why this is so: "I think the women's movement demonized some of the most valuable and worthwhile work in the world: making a home for the people who love you."

Moreover, she sees an ironic backlash from feminism's vilification of males. "Modern women have not been served well by the lingering contempt for men which has been an unfortunate byproduct of the women's movement." Feminism, "built on a powerful notion of liberation," has actually served to isolate the sexes, to create a cultural rift, an antagonism that inevitably has weakened society.

Relieving men of the twin obligations to protect and provide for women, this isolation of the sexes serves to encourage male irresponsibility, freeing men up to indulge in selfish pursuits, often ones that drive the wedge of gender isolation still deeper. Addiction to pornography and the legitimizing of homosexuality have contributed to the breakdown of the family and the fallout of single-parent homes. Not only has this backlash hurt women (the "single parent" in most of those homes: remember my log-truck driver), it hurts the children, both male and female, who make up the next generation spiraling into despair as a result of feminism's errors.

Happy or not, smart, successful women have achieved their autonomy from men, so feminists insist. But it's autonomy with a downside. Men are not exactly lining up to marry many of these self-styled smart, successful women. Feminists are sure it's because the male of the species just isn't up to snuff for real liberated women.

Syndicated columnist Kathleen Parker offers another reason: "Men haven't turned away from smart, successful women because they're smart and successful. They've turned away because the feminist movement that encouraged women to be smart and successful also encouraged them to be hostile and demeaning to men." Not a good attitude on which to build a marriage—or a healthy society.

"When we're not bashing men," Parker continues, "we're diminishing manhood. Look around at entertainment and other cultural signposts and you see a feminized culture that prefers sanitized men—

hairless, coiffed, buffed, and, if possible, gay." Nobody wins in a society built on that kind of social expectation. The tragicomedy of it all—women themselves lose the most.

"Feminism failed to recognize," Parker laments, "that even smart, successful women also want to be mothers. It's called Nature. Social engineering can no more change that fact than mechanical engineering can change the laws of Physics." She concludes without equivocation, "The feminist movement was a hoax."

Mansfield agrees. Sounding more like one of the seventeenth-century Puritans who founded Harvard than a modern who teaches there, Professor Mansfield concludes, "To a woman, home is where your husband lives and where your children learn. For the great majority of human beings, happiness is found in a happy home. To be the manager of a home is the moderate and attainable ambition of most women; it is the place where they find honor and joy."

And it is this home happiness that feminism labors to destroy, a labor that has, alas, been profoundly successful. "The eradication of men and fathers from children's lives" is what Kathleen Parker calls "feminism's most despicable accomplishment." She blames feminism for the fact that "half of all children will sleep tonight in a home where their father does not live." And maybe where they have a mom who drives a log truck and wishes she didn't have to.

Death of Modesty

Combine Betty Friedan's 1963 book with the sexual revolution, and you have the imploding formula for dismantling moral decency. The liberated Friedan feminist tore off her female foundation wear and paraded in the streets with a message that went like this: "We can be as promiscuous as men; watch and see!" Thus, as feminism set about redefining female virtue, modesty became the vice to shun, while the virtues to strive after became promiscuity and brazen immodesty.

Under the feminist cloud deconstructing morality, pornography proliferated. Friedan feminism ensured that there would be plenty of models for the cameras, and the invention of the World Wide Web in 1989 ensured that there'd be millions of dupes lining up to neuter themselves on the cyber road to death.

Internet technology, wrote R. C. Sproul Jr., "carpet bombed the last great defense against sexual perversion, shame. The Internet is the first pornography delivery system that doesn't require any interaction with a live human being. Public shame is now gone." Young men who value life must never take the first step down the porn path to death. Author Jennifer Schneider gives the reason: "The internet is the crack cocaine of sexual addiction." Some studies indicate that an astounding 90 percent of Internet use is for pornography.

Clearly, a society saturated with effortless pornography is going to have an increasingly difficult time defining modesty.

Modesty is a moving target as each cultural value change lowers the threshold of what is appropriate public clothing. It would be an enormous mistake, however, to assume that radical feminists parading in the streets and swinging their brassieres are the only ones defying feminine modesty. Cultural values always affect fashion, and this is the case with the new reversal of values dictated by feminism.

Unknowingly many Christian young women have joined Friedan feminists by abandoning virtue in what they wear. I've heard Christians defend immodest female clothing as though the Bible said nothing about a woman who "dressed like a prostitute" (Prov. 7:10), whose "slain are a mighty throng" (7:26b). Or they view feminine fashion as though Paul never penned the words, "I also want women to dress modestly, with decency and propriety" (1 Tim. 2:9).

Christian women who strut to church in backless dresses, spaghetti straps, short skirts, and plunging necklines not only make themselves objects of lust to males, but unwittingly support the conclusions of feminists who liberated themselves from modesty. They don't stop to consider the impression they're making on teen males, or on the single adult Christian male who struggles every day with longing for a wife—a struggle that may quickly descend into lusting after someone else's.

Feminization of Church

This ubiquitous feminization of society has made its way perniciously into the church. Sermons, once doctrinal expositions of God's Word to his church, have become roving self-help chit-chats offering Oprah-like advice on how biblical principles will make your relationships more fulfilling.

Predictably, the feminist attack on Christianity levels its sights on biblical patriarchy in church leadership. On cue, once-conservative, Bible-believing churches now accommodate feminism by ordaining female elders and pastors.

Liberal denominations have opened their arms to the feminists, but may have gotten more than they bargained for; half the elders in the Presbyterian Church USA are women, and 75 percent of membership is female—and aging. Made up predominantly of old ladies, most liberal churches are not places where men want to hang out. Post-conservative evangelical churches are not far behind, with 64 percent female attendees.

Some ministers give up ground to the feminization of Christianity by scrupulously encumbering their delivery with gender-inclusive language. Jim Elliot's memorable lines on self-sacrifice become a mush-mouth of proliferated pronouns: "He or she is no fool who gives what he or she cannot keep to gain what he or she cannot lose." Nobody would think to quote Elliot if he'd obscured his meaning by hashing the language that way.

If the preaching of the Word of God is the Word of God, then real men are obligated by the language of that Word to speak as the Bible speaks. "He who believes in me will live, even though he dies" (John 11:25), Jesus said—speaking to a woman. Ministers who accommodate feminism by using gender-inclusive language train a generation of young people to find the language of the Bible increasingly odd, a generation that will be happy to jettison the God-breathed language of the Bible for a gender-inclusive paraphrase.

Feminism also tells young men how to be spiritual: act like women. "Come to church first and foremost to feel," feminized Christianity tells you, "not to think." Thus, the new feminized liturgy is emotive, experiential, and touchy-feely. Singing is breathy and sentimental, with little doctrinal content.

Men who write music and sway on the stage with the women worship leaders are often effeminate men who have bought in bulk what feminism has been peddling to the church. They sing with slack jaw, eyes half-closed, hands caressing the air—like the women—as they croon out the latest entertainment nonsense that passes for worship songs.

Contemporary worship is shaped by women, not by real men. But you do not have to act like a woman to be a Christian man. In fact, you *must not* act like a woman if you are to be a real Christian man. Beware and hold fast against feminized worship.

Masculinity Defined

But exactly what does it mean to be a man? While feminism destroys humanity by abolishing masculinity, how does a Christian young man resist the pressure to become what it wants you to become: limp-wristed, compliant, and nonpatriarchal?

Like all other cultural delusions, feminism doesn't work because it is a radical departure from the Bible. To fix the problem, you must return to the Word of God. "Be on your guard; stand firm in the faith; be men of courage; be strong. Do everything in love" (1 Cor. 16:13–14).

Real men live on guard, hands on their weapons, eyes scanning the horizon. A watchful young man must forgo some things. He must stand apart for the good of the whole. And a watchful man is self-controlled. While others frolic, the watchful young man stands guard, at the ready, protecting the weak and vulnerable around him. God calls you to watchfulness.

Real men hold fast by standing firm against the enemy of their souls. When the enemy charges, however terrifying he appears, a real man stands his ground. He may be afraid; standing firm may cost him his life. But he doesn't turn and run. A man of courage stands firm.

A real man is a strong man. There's much more to strength, however, than bench-pressing at the gym. However buff you are when you're eighteen, there'll come a time when you must face the reality of your own weakness.

The fact is: "Even youths grow tired and weary, and young men stumble and fall; but those who hope in the LORD will renew their strength" (Isa. 40:30–31a). This is the strength Paul is getting at. Real strength comes to the man who hopes in the Lord's strength, not in his own.

Finally, biblical masculinity requires you to do everything in love. Men are called to protect and provide for their wives and children, and they are called to do this out of Christlike love.

Feminists, who attempt to act like men while forbidding men to act like men, hate this definition of masculinity. They hate the notion that men are to use their strength to serve God and others in Christ's name.

Because feminism defies God's created order, it is doomed to failure, but it takes many casualties on the way. God made humans male and female, and he gave specific roles to each. Out of love for God and your neighbor—male and female—hold fast to your role. Be a man.

Prayer Resolves

- To cultivate speech, mannerisms, and posture in keeping with my role as a man
- To cultivate biblical strength and use it for others

Scripture Memory

"Husbands, live with your wives in an understanding way, showing honor to the woman as the weaker vessel."

1 Peter 3:7 (ESV)

For Discussion

1. In what ways does feminism facilitate male irresponsibility?
2. How can you help others in your life to fulfill their roles as men and women?

"The Lord, Great Sovereign"

He makes his children mighty men;
    They bend the battle bow.
So in God's strength, against the proud,
    His foes they overthrow.

Douglas Bond, 2001

For Further Study

Proverbs 31; Ephesians 5

15

MARRIAGE
DECONSTRUCTED

Genesis 2:19–25; Ephesians 5:31–32

"What's wrong with lawyer jokes? Lawyers don't think they're funny, and the rest of us don't think they're jokes." We've all guffawed at good lawyer jokes. But Steven T. O'Ban's work as an attorney is no laughing matter. Designated a "Super Lawyer" in the magazine Law & Politics, *Steve has more than once been recognized by his peers as being in the top 5 percent of practicing attorneys. He works for the preeminent Seattle-based firm representing nonprofits and other religious organizations in First Amendment cases. In one high-profile case, Steve appeared on* Good Morning America *while defending the rights of Protestant churches and pastors. Before the U.S. Supreme Court, Steve defended the right of workers not to be compelled to contribute to political and ideological causes they oppose. In a case nearly everyone expected him to lose, Steve successfully argued before the Washington State Supreme Court to uphold traditional marriage from attacks by the ACLU and homosexual-rights groups.*

Spouse A and Spouse B

Few cultural issues represent a greater challenge to biblical truth than the campaign to legalize homosexual marriage. Even so, why do a father and his son need to discuss this issue together? After all, if you're reading this book, you probably aren't planning to go out and marry someone of the same sex. But how others think of and practice marriage does affect us. Perhaps no better example is another watershed alteration to marriage that did become law—so-called no-fault divorce. This monumental change permitted either spouse to dissolve the marriage for any reason, stripping away from marriage the expectation of permanence and stability. Marriage has never been the same since, including, sadly, many Christian marriages.

Why Should You Care?

Marriage as defined by government, practiced by our neighbors, and celebrated by our culture will impact the way you think of marriage and shape the society in which you will live as an adult. We should know what we believe about marriage because it is not a social construct invented by man. It was created by God for our good and mysteriously symbolizes the relationship between Christ and his church (Gen. 2:19–25; Eph. 5:31–32).

The current debate focuses on civil marriage, not religious marriage. Homosexual-marriage advocates want to change the definition of civil marriage, not, at least at this point, marriage solemnized by the church. Gays cast marriage as a merely private arrangement. They say any two people committed to each other should be allowed to marry. Gays try to ignore the fact that marriage weaves into the fabric of society its very character. Marriage, Christian and pagan, is society's fundamental organizing unit.

Marriage is the superstructure on which the family is built. Through marriage and the family, beliefs and values are modeled and transmitted from one generation to the next. Such civic virtues as honesty, generosity, volunteerism, and patriotism—and their opposite vices—are formed and shaped in a family.

The most important ethic, because it animates all virtue, is uniquely practiced in marriage. Through marriage, opposites in sex, appearance, body structure, and outlook learn the unique differences of gender while also learning to appreciate and value how opposites can complement one another to achieve what alone each would be unable to achieve. Marriage is the paradigm by which God intended that society model selfless love.

Why Would Legalizing Homosexual Marriage Be Wrong?

Having shown that society's position on marriage is enormously important and worthy of our consideration, the next question is how would extending marriage to homosexuals undermine marriage? Some say that letting homosexuals marry might benefit society by making homosexuals live in more committed relationships.

But to answer this question, we need to go back to our Owner's manual, the Scriptures. When God first instituted marriage in Genesis 2, he could not have been more clear: "For this reason a *man* will leave his father and mother and be united to his *wife*, and they will become one flesh." No loopholes. Marriage is between a man and his wife. And even if this passage did not exist, God has condemned homosexuality in no uncertain terms (Rom. 1:26–28). It follows that if homosexual behavior is wrong, then endorsing homosexual relationships by recognizing and supporting them through civil marriage is unacceptable to God.

On the surface, the controversy appears to be about the rights of gays versus the true definition of civil marriage. But deep down, the real issue at stake is God's authority. The gay-marriage battle is nothing less than the creature's rejection of his Creator's right to define man and the basic social unit on which a healthy human society is constructed.

Another way of framing the struggle is that those who champion gay marriage deny that there is such a thing as human nature. If there is no fixed human nature, then no universal moral principles can be read from human nature. If there are no universal moral truths, then Christianity's God is merely a form of oppression and myth. Homosexual-marriage advocates are engaging in a particularly destructive, but certainly not new, form of fallen man's timeless campaign to displace God and exalt himself.

Same- and Opposite-Sex Unions Are Not Equal

Same-sex and opposite-sex unions are not equal in all sorts of ways, some so obvious that no comment is necessary, and some that should be obvious but are downplayed by the media. As measured by fidelity and longevity, there is no comparison. Based on a study conducted by a prominent gay publication, researchers concluded that the average same-sex female union lasted 4.9 years, the average same-sex male couple, 6.9 years, and the average heterosexual couple, 20 years. Homosexual partners are drawn to each other by sameness—for example, the same sexual interests and sexual attitudes. Relationships based simply on shared interests are less stable. And more significantly, homosexual behavior is sin, and no relationship that celebrates sin can expect to be deeply stable and satisfying.

To heterosexuals, however, sexual differences and complementariness are the powerful appeal. Most heterosexual couples value those differences and expect that they must learn to understand, accept, and adjust to them. In this way, key social virtues are practiced in the family because they are built into the heterosexual relationship: selflessness and respect for diversity. This is not to deny that many, many unhappy marriages are warped by selfishness. But the elements are present in a heterosexual union to encourage each spouse to value difference. The superiority of heterosexual marriage is no accident. God created marriage between a man and a woman, and said it was "good." Marriage of one man and one woman carries with it God's all-important blessing.

Why Do Gays and Lesbians Demand Marriage?

So if gay relationships are not conducive to lifelong marriage, why have gays made marriage their "holy grail," subordinating their other social and political goals to it? At a conference in which this author debated an influential gay-marriage advocate, she conceded that a short time ago most homosexuals disdained marriage as far too limiting. Why did gays change their mind? Homosexual-marriage advocates give the answer openly and without hesitation: they want the legitimacy that comes with the endorsement of a government-issued marriage license.

With such an official stamp of social approval, homosexual relationships and homosexual behaviors would become fully mainstreamed into all of American life. *Mainstreaming* means not just presenting openly homosexual men and women favorably, but eliminating moral and even social distinctions suggesting that heterosexual identity and behavior are to be preferred. After the Massachusetts Supreme Court mandated gay marriage, the government removed from its marriage certificate the identifiers *husband* and *wife*. In the Canadian province of Ontario, within two weeks of legalizing gay marriage, the government prohibited all its agencies and officials from using *husband* and *wife* and *father* and *mother*.

Right now, gay marriage in Massachusetts and several Canadian provinces is the exception. If gay marriage becomes the norm, gay and lesbian subculture would become inseparable from American culture. Though American culture has come to embrace homosexuality as never before, removing the key legal, political, and social barrier (the marriage limitation) would accelerate at light speed the normalization of homosexual behavior. Before long, no one but a "bigot" would make moral distinctions between homosexuals and heterosexuals. In other words, to label homosexuality as immoral would invite social disapproval, isolation, and censure.

Legal Battle or Culture War?

With so many states passing laws prohibiting gay marriage, why should we be concerned that it might one day become legal?

The Rev. Richard Neuhaus, editor-in-chief of the nation's best religious journal (*First Things*), wrote, "Thousands of ethicists, as they are called, professionally guide the unthinkable on its passage through the debatable on its way to becoming the justifiable, until it is finally established as the unexceptional."

Anyone over forty years old will tell you that when they were in high school, gay marriage was unthinkable. Now in many academic institutions, within the mainstream media, and in several Western countries, gay marriage is justifiable, if not unexceptional. Like all legal battles, the real battlefront is cultural. In democracies, laws change to reflect conventional wisdom and practice. Time is on the side of gay-marriage advocates. The ever-increasing acceptance of homosexual behavior shows no signs of abating.

We should take encouragement from the certain truth that most Americans currently feel that there are simply some nonnegotiables when it comes to tampering with such a vital social institution. At some level, most Americans believe the intrinsic nature of marriage springs from immutable gender differences of men and women. After all, only a man and a woman can unite to bear a child. But only a generation ago, most Americans believed openly homosexual men and women should not teach in schools or otherwise serve in positions in which they were role models for children. Now, in most states, homosexuals are free to adopt children and serve as foster parents.

No reader should be putting his confidence in a traditional-marriage amendment to the U.S. Constitution. The amendment process would take several years, requiring supermajority votes in the U.S. House of Representatives and Senate and approval by two-thirds of the states. The culture will decide this issue long before a constitutional amendment places it beyond the reach of the courts and legislatures.

Christians must confront the profound consequences at stake if the gay-marriage battle is lost. The existing social guardrails that keep the homosexual agenda from driving our culture over a cliff would be removed. We could expect more and more impressionable young people to accept homosexuality not just as a "valid lifestyle," but as the equivalent of heterosexuality. The damage would be great and irreversible. Legitimizing gay marriage is *the* equivalent of setting off a social nuclear bomb.

As Christians we naturally, and rightly, think of the persecution that would result. Right now, the vitriol against Christians who take a stand in the public square against the homosexual agenda and similar cultural issues is commonplace. We know the persecution would get worse. Our Savior told us to expect such persecution and that he would strengthen us (Matt. 5:11–12). He gave us a magnificent example of how to bear up under it (Isa. 53:7).

Our chief concern, however, is not for our own fate, but that of the lost. Christ showed us that the eternal fate of his persecutors was uppermost in his mind (Matt. 23:37; Luke 23:34).

The reasons that Christians want to protect God's institution of marriage and confront the agenda of gay-marriage advocates are the same reasons our Lord gave us for all our life's work: to love God and love our neighbor. We want to honor his truth and his authority as Creator and King of his creation and to warn our countrymen that gay marriage and mainstreaming gay relationships and behavior will bring pain, broken relationships, shattered lives, eternal ruin.

How to Protect Marriage

The first step in protecting marriage is to own up to our part in helping to bring it down. Homosexuals were not the first to dig away at the foundations of marriage. In fact, gay-marriage advocates are meeting with some success only because heterosexuals began to undermine it decades ago. Social scientists tell us that nearly one in two marriages will end in divorce. As one judge stated in his decision in favor of gay marriage, the greatest threat to marriage is not from without (by gays), but from within marriage itself.

Although the claim that divorce is as rampant in the evangelical church as the society around it is exaggerated, no one can deny that Christians divorce at rates that belie our rhetorical support for biblical marriage. Historically, God's people are called to be holy, and to the extent they have been, the unsaved were changed for the better and society and culture benefited. So if you really want to get at the root cause of the instability of the institution of marriage, you must ask yourself what you really believe about marriage. Ask: How important are the marriage vows I someday will take? What steps must I take to make sure I marry for life?

In addition to walking the talk, another important step for Christian young men obeying the biblical injunction to engage their culture is to be prepared to assure others, winsomely and yet frankly, that absolutes do still exist. We know all too well that American culture has embraced relativism—"What is right for you may not be right for me." Even otherwise intelligent Americans now accept this slogan uncritically. A recent U.S. Supreme Court case held that a majority of citizens through their elected representatives could no longer enact laws to prohibit behavior purely because they thought it was wrong.

And yet no one really believes that relativism is true, since it contradicts reality. Everyone holds to some absolute, fixed truths: "Murder is wrong," "Harming the environment is wrong," "Taking my hairbrush, without asking me first, is wrong." No one genuinely thinks murdering, torching a warehouse for kicks, dumping crude oil in the ocean, or stealing a car is wrong for some but perfectly okay for others.

Our neighbors, friends, and workmates need to hear us say, with both graciousness and firmness, that homosexuality is destructive, unhealthy, and dehumanizing. It is wrong. And because homosexual behavior is wrong, endorsing homosexual relationships by calling them *marriage* is just as wrong.

Finally, we must be able to explain biblical morality in prudential terms. Most Americans do not read the Bible because they do not accept it as the standard by which they ought to live. We must be able to persuade others based on grounds that demonstrate that God's will for his creatures is not only right morally, but also for their best.

Prayer Resolves

- To cultivate sexual purity in thoughts, words, and deeds
- To pray for the salvation of homosexuals, especially their influential leaders
- To understand and practice Christian masculinity

Scripture Memory

"Because of this, God gave them over to shameful lusts. Even their women exchanged natural relations for unnatural ones. In the same way the men also abandoned natural relations with women and were inflamed with lust for one another. Men committed indecent acts with other men, and received in themselves the due penalty for their perversion."

Romans 1:26–27

For Discussion

1. What steps must you be taking now in order to marry for life someday?
2. What steps should you be taking to ensure purity of mind and affections?
3. How should you as a Christian think and speak about homosexuals?

"The Sands of Time Are Sinking"

The bride eyes not her garment,
But her dear bridegroom's face;
I will not gaze at glory,
But on my King of grace.

Anne R. Cousin, 1857

For Further Study

Genesis 18:16–19:29; Leviticus 18:22; 20:13

16

DELIVER US FROM EVIL

Psalm 139:13–18

My friend John Chaffee is the kind of man I'd want to have at my side if I were really sick. Why is this? Dr. Chaffee is a Christian physician who knows the grace of God personally and lives it out in his life and work. He has dedicated himself to lifelong learning, to providing excellent medical care to his patients, and to teaching young medical professionals. He received his medical degree from Harvard Medical School, and was recently awarded the distinguished Degree of Fellow by the Academy of Family Physicians; he is an assistant clinical professor at the University of Washington. His research has been published, including in the Journal of Family Practice. *Dr. Chaffee was a one-time president of the Harvard Chapter of the Christian Medical Association, where as a current member he labors in the pro-life trenches. He is supported in this work by his wife and four children.*

About to Deliver

"Doctor, come now!" The nurse's voice was anxious. "She is about to deliver."

"I'll be right up," I said.

Sharon had labored through the evening. As I headed to the OB floor, I thought about Sharon and her husband, Ken—what a lovely couple! I had enjoyed attending their wedding. Ken had gotten to know Sharon and her family first through friendship and then courtship. He had been respectful and self-controlled. They had kept themselves for each other. Sharon basked in the security of her marriage and, though she had prolonged morning sickness, had always been excited about bringing a child into their family.

I bounded up the hospital stairwell. As I passed the waiting room, expectant grandparents locked their eyes on me, ready to eject from their chairs. Once I was through the doors of the obstetric ward, things were buzzing.

"Room Four," a nurse called out. Ken was at Sharon's bedside, holding her hand. He spoke tenderly to her, encouraging her through a painful contraction. Sharon's face reflected back his confidence.

"Sharon, how are you handling the pain?" I asked.

"Okay for now," she replied, closing her eyes and resting against the pillow.

After listening to Sharon's heart and lungs with my stethoscope, I confirmed the normal position of the baby's head for this stage of the delivery. The baby's head moved down with the next contraction. In the background the fetal heart monitor drummed out the baby's heart rate, graphing it along with the contractions. The tracing was normal.

"How much longer?" Sharon asked.

"It won't be long. Your baby seems to be doing fine," I said, checking the equipment at the infant warmer to make sure that all was working and ready to use in case of an emergency.

I reflected on the moment. In Genesis we are told that "God created man in his own image . . . ; male and female he created them. God blessed them and said to them, 'Be fruitful and increase in number; fill the earth and subdue it' " (Gen. 1:27–28). In his wonderful wisdom, God instituted marriage for a man and a woman to be united for life, to bring forth children and raise them with love and discipline in the secure environment of a family.

Sharon's breathing became heavier. The nurse pulled the drape from the table, exposing a sterile gown, gloves, and delivery instruments. I slid my arms into the sleeves of the gown as the nurse tied it from behind. Looking around the room, I was reminded of what a great privilege it is to be a physician.

With Sharon's next contraction the drumming of the baby's heart rate slowed from the usual 130s to 110, then to 90. This got my attention. I mentally went through the possibilities and steps I might need to take. Just as my adrenaline began to flow, the baby's heart rate came up again, which suggested that the drop was due to pressure on the baby's head or possibly a loop of umbilical cord around the neck. I offered a silent prayer for a safe delivery and for wisdom for the nurses and myself.

Pro-Life

In 1973 the U.S. Supreme Court *Roe v. Wade* decision legalized abortion in America, sweeping away laws in nearly all fifty states against it. In order to support their decision, the majority of justices stepped out of their judicial role, making basic biological and theological judgments about when life begins. By voting to legalize abortion, they ruled that either life does not begin at conception or, if it does, it somehow no longer matters.

The beginning of a new life, however, is not a matter of judicial opinion. When a seed from a man and an egg from a woman are joined into a single cell, a new human life begins. Every new human life, so conceived, bears the image of God and is of great importance.

Consider the following. That first living cell has the complete genetic code for a unique human being, already male or female. A nine-week-old baby in the womb has a heartbeat and circulatory system, a respiratory system, eyes, ears, and brain function. He can squint, swallow, and make a fist. At twenty weeks, he can cry, smile, and frown. All this happens whether he is wanted or unwanted, whether the parents are married or unmarried.

There is no time in our lives, including the time from conception in the womb, when God does not care for us and when life should not be protected. King David wrote, "For you created my inmost being; you knit me together in my mother's womb. I praise you because I am fearfully and wonderfully made" (Ps. 139:13–14a). God's law in the sixth commandment spells it out: "You shall not murder" (Ex. 20:13). Hence, taking a human life, especially that of a baby in the womb, is profoundly evil.

Ill-Conceived

Unlike the joy that Ken and Sharon had at the news that they were expecting a child, many women today receive the news of their pregnancy with dread, panic, even anger. Alas, the United States has the highest adolescent pregnancy rates and, correspondingly, the highest abortion rates in the world. Almost a million American teenage girls become pregnant every year. What is more, 78 percent of births to teens occur outside of marriage. How did this come about?

In the 1960s the sexual revolution broke out with development of the birth-control pill (13 percent still get pregnant) concurrent with a nationwide movement through the media and music, promoting rebellion against authority and "free love," sex outside of marriage, in defiance of God's law. Concurrently, pornography exploded, depicting women as passing objects of sexual pleasure. Today, pornography in various forms saturates advertisement, entertainment, and cyberspace. The result is the debasing of both men and women.

Compound the sexual revolution with radical feminism, and the problem becomes more intractable. Feminists made a mockery of modesty, courtship, and sexual purity. As an essential part of liberating women, they promoted sex without regard for the marriage commitment. They scorned the role of mother as homemaker and father as leader, provider, and protector of women and children in the home. Feminists achieved legal sanction for their attack on biblical manhood and womanhood and the family with the passage of the "no-fault divorce" law of 1970, further undermining marriage as a lifelong commitment.

Pro-Death

Abortion activists insist that abortion on demand is a woman's basic right and is needed for women to gain absolute control over human reproduction. Guided by moral relativism, they discourage self-control or abstinence as the primary means for preventing teen pregnancy. Abortion activists have shaped the argument by insisting that what a woman does with her body is her "choice." This choice has resulted in more than forty-seven million babies being aborted in our country since legalization of abortion in 1973. Nearly every third baby is killed by abortion. One life conceived in the image of God is ended every twenty-five seconds.

In abortion a physician and a woman become coconspirators by entering a most protected and private area of her body, there to end a life. The abortionist violates that sacred place of nurture and protection by forcing a woman's unripe womb to open. For early abortions, a sharp-tipped vacuum is inserted. What follows is brutal in the extreme. The psalmist wrote that God's eyes *"saw my unformed body"* (Ps. 139:16).

In later pregnancies, the abortionist uses steel instruments to dismember the body and crush the skull of the baby in the womb in order to remove it more easily. The psalmist wrote, *"My frame was not hidden from you when I was made in the secret place"* (v. 15a).

In partial-birth abortion, done in late pregnancy, part of a living baby is intentionally delivered for the purpose of killing the baby before completing the delivery—all without regard for the baby's pain. Nearly fifty thousand partial-birth abortions have been performed in the last decade, most by a few dozen abortionists. Obstetric experts have testified before Congress that the procedure is *never* necessary for the health of the mother. Most partial-birth abortions are purely elective or done to avoid surgically correctable conditions such as cleft lip or palate.

Not only does abortion destroy the life of a child; it hurts women, and in many cases destroys their lives. Risks from the procedure itself include infection, infertility, and even death. Women who have had abortions are three times more likely to commit suicide than the general population and are six times more likely to take their own lives than women who give birth to their babies.

At the last, abortion hardens men and women to the value of life and is a disgrace to the medical profession. The U.S. Supreme Court has recently upheld the federal law criminalizing partial-birth abortion based on the fact that it is never medically necessary for the health of the mother. The truth is that abortion is only very rarely medically justifiable at any point in pregnancy. Like William Wilberforce, who prepared himself and stood effectively and persistently against slavery, the evil of his day, it falls to you and to your generation to turn back this tide of evil and to protect life.

Love Grows Cold

Abortion has led to a numbing coldness toward life. How could it do otherwise? And the most vulnerable—the unborn, the elderly, and the infirm—are at greatest risk.

Doctors routinely perform tests on pregnant women to detect genetic traits such as Down syndrome, cystic fibrosis, and sickle-cell disease. Tragically, these tests are usually obtained as a prelude to counseling women to abort, the easy way to be rid of the imperfect child. Testing is even done for the purpose of identifying and aborting perfectly normal female babies.

Moreover, human embryos are being sacrificed in *embryonic* stem-cell research even though not a single effective treatment or cure has been produced by this type of research. In contrast, *adult* stem-cell research does not require the taking of a life and has produced treatments and cures for seventy diseases, and is likely to produce a cure for diabetes in the very near future.

Like abortion, physician-assisted suicide is an attack on life, a direct violation of the Hippocratic oath, the ancient moral code whereby physicians swore not to take part in abortion or suicide. Yet physician-assisted suicide has been legalized in Oregon and is gaining support in other states. Euthanasia, so-called mercy killing, has been legalized in Holland, where an average of three patients a day are killed by doctors *without* the patients' consent or knowledge, including patients with treatable conditions.

Sexual Purity and Life

The Bible is frank about sexual matters—and about the consequences. "Flee also youthful lusts: but follow righteousness . . ." (2 Tim. 2:22 KJV). *Flee* means "to get away"—run, even if you have to leave your coat, as Joseph did from Potiphar's wife.

Yours is a culture saturated with pornography. Sexually alluring images appear all around you, and they're designed to hit you at times and places where you are vulnerable. You must constantly guard your eyes, ears, and mind if you are to keep your spiritual strength.

Young men must be absolutely clear about sexual purity. "Do not be deceived: God cannot be mocked. A man reaps what he sows. The one who sows to please his sinful nature, from that nature will reap destruction; the one who sows to please the Spirit, from the Spirit will reap eternal life" (Gal. 6:7–8).

God designed sexual intimacy between a husband and wife not only for procreation, to make babies, but also for pleasure. Let's be honest—every young man feels the pull toward that pleasure. Just as God fashioned your body in your mother's womb, so he designed you with the powerful desire for sexual pleasure, but it will be enduring pleasure only within the boundaries that God has ordained.

A young man prepares himself for a happy, satisfying, and fruitful marriage by committing himself now to a life of sexual purity and self-control, to a life of obedience to God. Be guided by the inseparable character of love and faithfulness in marriage as in all of life. "Let love and faithfulness never leave you; bind them around your neck, write them on the tablet of your heart. Then you will win favor and a good name in the sight of God and man" (Prov. 3:3–4).

The Way It's Supposed to Be

"The pressure is coming again," Sharon said, breaking the silence.

She took a deep breath and pushed. Ken assisted her, counting out loud to ten. The very top of the baby's head became visible, rotating back and forth. Sharon let out a long breath and closed her eyes. All was silent but the drumming of the monitor. Ken grasped Sharon's hand, watching alertly over her, praying silently. He was not alone. Time seemed to stand still. I arranged the instruments in the order of use for the delivery. The nurses stood ready, one at the bedside and the other at the infant warmer.

"Sharon, I want you to push with your next contraction," I said. "When I ask you to stop pushing, just breathe like you are blowing out a candle so I can suction your baby before its first breath."

Sharon nodded her head in understanding. Moments later her breathing became heavier with the contraction, like a train building up steam. She took a deep breath and started to push. She let out a long, moaning cry. The top of the baby's head began to emerge—first the brow, then the closed eyes, the nose, the mouth, and then the chin.

"Sharon, stop pushing and breathe," I said firmly, taking the suction bulb and removing fluid from the mouth and the nose. Then sliding my hand over the back of the baby's head to the nape, I detected a loop of umbilical cord around the baby's neck. It easily slipped forward over the baby's head. "Sharon, now it is time to have your baby."

Sharon held her breath and pushed. With my hands supporting the baby's head, I directed the baby's course of delivery. I turned the baby over, holding her securely. "A girl," I announced. The baby's arms reached out widely and upward, which always reminds me of a gesture of praise. Then with a great heave of her tiny chest, the baby drew in her first breath and let out an explosive cry.

This little girl had gone from receiving all her oxygenated blood through the umbilical cord to breathing air, but was otherwise the same little girl, still completely dependent. As I held her, I watched the bluish hue of her skin turn to a bright pink as she cried. I felt that same urge to praise whelming up inside of me.

Her first little breath was joined by many sighs of relief. Every anticipation was met, and every worry of danger dispelled, with that beautiful cry. I clamped the umbilical cord and handed the scissors to her father to cut her loose. Tears welled up from many eyes. Ken let out unrestrained exclamations of joy, so proud and beaming. Grandparents eagerly burst into the room to catch a first glimpse.

I placed the baby on the mother's abdomen, where she made a crawling movement up to the breast, with help from her tearful but wonderfully satisfied mother. The nurses continued to dry the baby with towels as Sharon and Ken, now cheek to cheek, peered together for the first time at the tiny face of this long-awaited and precious life.

With gratitude and humility, I reflected on the wonder of life. This was birth; this was the way a new life is to enter the world as God ordained it from the beginning of time. This is the way it's supposed to be.

Prayer Resolves

- To commit myself to sexual purity in mind and body
- To avoid all occasions of lust, including all forms of pornography
- To pursue protecting the elderly, the unborn, and women and children

Scripture Memory

"Defend the cause of the weak and fatherless; maintain the rights of the poor and oppressed. Rescue the weak and needy; deliver them from the hand of the wicked."

Psalm 82:3–4

For Discussion

1. How is abortion like sacrificing infants to Molech (Lev. 20:1–5)?
2. Is "free love" really free? Who suffers from sex outside of marriage?
3. Why is conception the beginning of life?
4. How can a young man protect the elderly, the unborn, and women and children?

"Purer in Heart, O God"

Purer in heart, O God, help me to be;
May I devote my life wholly to thee:
Watch thou my wayward feet,
Guide me with counsel sweet;
Purer in heart, help me to be.

Fannie E. Davison, 1877

For Further Study

Psalm 139; Genesis 39

YOUNG MEN: DEATH, SUFFERING, AND HEAVEN

17

DADS, SONS, AND DEATH

Psalm 90

The Dreaded Phone Call

"If I ever get on my feet again"—my father's voice was faint, but his tone was firm and resolved—"I'm going to visit more sick folks in the hospital." Odd words coming from a man suffering with the rare combination of myelodysplastic syndrome and acute myelogenous leukemia, who wanted more than anything to get out of hospitals.

I will never forget that first telephone call from my mother five months earlier. They had known for two months that something was not right.

"We didn't want you to worry," my mother explained in her everything-is-going-to-be-okay voice. "After all, it may be nothing. But your dad's blood work—it's not quite what it ought to be. They've been tracking things pretty carefully since January."

I had learned to sense through this kind of studied calmness that deeper things lurked beneath, though it would be several weeks before she let me in on her real fears.

"For some reason they haven't quite figured out yet," she continued, "your dad's platelets, white cells, red cells—everything—they just keep going down, down, down."

She handed the phone to my dad. We talked for several minutes. I remember that he didn't sound any different. I thought he should sound different. Then, in his enthusiastic math-teacher voice, he told me about the graphs he had developed to track his plummeting blood cells. Later, he showed me the graphs, laying them end to end on the hood of his car. To me they were mocking and inhuman, jagged red lines plunging like lemmings off the last page. I gazed wide-eyed and tried to swallow the lump caught in my throat.

"This all means," he said, his voice leveling to a monotone, "that my bone marrow is a bit confused."

I looked from the graphs to my father. He looked fine to me: tall, slender, energetic in a patient, dignified way. How could he be so sick?

Young and Healthy—for Now

You're young and, I hope, healthy. Though your dad may have developed bulges in places where there used to be rock-hard muscle, and you like to poke at and crack jokes about those places, he's probably still in good health—for now. You may, however, know another young man whose father became seriously ill and may have died from that illness. So had I.

But I had never felt this tightness in my chest, this cowering unease. Now it was my own father. Numbness settled over me. It seemed as though none of this should be happening.

For six anxious weeks my father underwent chemotherapy, six weeks of spiking fevers, fungal pneumonia, rigors, nausea, delirium, six weeks for me of going in and out of the doors of St. Joseph's Hospital, often several times a day or night. My father had always taken care of me when I was young. Even as an adult, I had looked to him for wisdom and strength. With that phone call, all that had changed.

Prepare yourself, young man. Someday your father will need you more than you can fully know right now. Someday you will need him more than you think you do right now.

Sick as he was, my father needed the strength of his family to bear the weight of his disease. My father now needed my physical strength to do for him what he used to be able to do for himself. At critical times, he needed my emotional and spiritual strength when his own was exhausted. Several times during those weeks my father gripped my hand and said with feeling, "Thank you for being here with me through this." I felt so inadequate, as though I ought to do more, that I owed him everything but had returned so little.

You are young and strong—for the moment. But the psalmist says that our days "quickly pass, and we fly away" (Ps. 90:10), that young men spring up like new grass but that "by evening it is dry and withered" (v. 6). You and I don't like that. We want to live forever. We were made to live forever. But when a loved one grows sick and dies, the numbing reality of our own death comes close—too close. As he suffered, my father taught me how to prepare for it all. Every day he did this.

My mother told me that when they had first heard the news, my father wanted to pray. Sure, he prayed that he would get well, but his highest concern was that he would never dishonor the Lord, that, come what may, he would honor Christ at every stage of his illness. We had no idea the extent to which this longing would be put to the test. While watching that testing, I came to appreciate more than ever the importance of generational faithfulness to the gospel.

"Throughout All Generations"

My father traced his family back to West Putford, Devonshire, England, where his ship's carpenter great-great-grandfather, John Wesley Bond, was born in 1809. I have an uncle, a great-uncle, and a great-grandfather who bear the name Charles Wesley Bond. Like his forebears, my father has grown up reading and memorizing Holy Scripture, praying, worshiping, and singing the great hymns of historic Christianity, and he has taught his children to do the same. So when his body was racked with pain and nausea, when he had trouble breathing, or when he was delirious, what came from his mouth was prayer and praise. "O, Lord, our Lord, how excellent is thy name in all the earth," he whispered at one particularly low point. At another he recited his favorite psalm: "Serve the LORD with gladness; come before his presence with singing." At still another he gripped my hand and cried out for me to "pray for strength!"

I sat in wonder many times at the strength the Lord gave him when he was too weak in body to lift a hand. Unlike many sick people, my father had so much strength to draw on, so much spiritual discipline and depth that others lack. I am deeply grateful for this, but I know that to have spiritual muscle at death, one must start building it while young and vigorous. For you, young man, that is right now. Someday you will need this strength. You must build it now.

The contemplation of being "dry and withered" bothers men, especially young ones in the morning of their lives. Sitting by my father's bed forced me to think of my own decay and death. Seeing my father pale and helpless on that bed shattered my self-deception. It is forcing me to "number [my] days aright" (Ps. 90:12).

Sickness and Lying

Gaining "a heart of wisdom" (Ps. 90:12) this way is not easy. Why do we squirm at the needles, the pulsing warbles of the machines that monitor the medications? Why do we stumble and grope for words? Why do we lie? "You're sure looking good. I just have a feeling that everything's going to be all right."

With medical technology making wonderful advances almost daily, we actually operate under the delusion that modern medicine can cure anything. Our emotions encourage us here. We hope; we want it to be true. Against all reason, in the greatest extremity of suffering and imminent death, we still delude ourselves. C. S. Lewis makes us stare uncomfortably at this human inclination when he has the demon Screwtape describe how much better for their "Father Below" when people grow sick "amid doctors who lie, nurses who lie, friends who lie, as we [the demons] have trained them, promising life to the dying." Better for the devil, however, is emphatically not better for your dying loved one—or for you.

I wonder if you and I don't adopt this posture of self-deception because, by convincing ourselves that the person lying on that bed will recover, we can delude ourselves into imagining that we will somehow be able to stay one step ahead of a disease that hovers on our own horizon waiting to overwhelm us.

When this line of reasoning crumbles, we begin constructing a *quid pro quo* argument that explains why that person deserved to get sick—but we don't. Though we would never admit to thinking this way, the raw nerve of our pride becomes exposed here. We'd never say, would we, "What do you expect from a guy who smoked? or who drank too much? or who refused to wear his seat belt, or take his vitamins, or eat his broccoli?" You and I are desperate to live forever, to be strong and vigorous. Death is fine for other folks, but it's not going to catch up with me. Maybe as a young man you imagine that growing old and sick and dying is so far out there—"a thousand years in your sight" (Ps. 90:4)—it's as if it will never really happen.

Hollywood Helps Us Amuse Ourselves to Death

Meanwhile, repulsed as we are by sickness, pain, and death, death holds a certain fascination for us—so long as we can detach it from our own experience. But this very detachment produces the problem.

In so many ways the media contributes to our distorted ideas about what death is, to our desperate struggle to spin it into something other than the cold intruder that it is. Joe Sehee, director of new development at Hollywood Forever Funeral Home, candidly admits that people believe that "with enough trips to the gym and plastic surgery, death is something that can be denied or cheated." Nevertheless, in the same breath he insists that "death is natural and we have to understand it and embrace it—and maybe even have fun with it." So funerals have become choreographed premiere documentaries on the life of the deceased, complete with props, DVDs, margaritas, and live butterflies released into the sky on cue from the producer.

With all of this extravagant whistling in the dark, we attempt to blunt the harsh realities, the "trouble and sorrow" (Ps. 90:10) of sickness and death. After all, we are entirely too busy pursuing the frivolities of contemporary life to willingly put ourselves in the way of the kind of sobering contemplation that results from sitting at the deathbed of someone we love.

Still more, maybe we are *Amusing Ourselves to Death*, as the title of a Neil Postman book poignantly asserts. Few deny that filmmakers and the news media have shaped death and suffering into vehicles of sensationalism and entertainment. Why? Because they have a voracious market. We desperately want it all to be merely special effects that give us a rush of adrenaline—but nothing more.

Ironically, the more we see staged human suffering, the more it inures us to the real thing, the more it pushes it away from our own lives, from our own deaths. The touted realism of twenty-seven minutes of special-effects human slaughter on French beaches backfires for most. This brand of realism, overwhelmed by the entertainment venue, finally makes death less real. Media exploitation of our fascination with death merely facilitates our eager inclination to not think soberly and personally about it, and thus not to "number our days aright" (Ps. 90:12).

Cheat Death and Live!

Undeniable clarity settles in, however, when we stare into the pain-blanched face of a real person who is really sick. Death is a monstrous intruder for which you and I have nothing but utter abhorrence. Why? Because we were made not for death but for life. Life was the result of creation, death the result of sin. But this predisposition in favor of life sometimes makes us grasp at any puff of hope, to cling to this life as if it were the real life. As Isaac Watts put it, "Timorous mortals start and shrink to cross the narrow sea." We recoil from death as if it were the final end, as if we were merely lumps of matter, dust that returns to the dust from which it came. Though no theologian, even Henry Wadsworth Longfellow in his "Psalm of Life" saw through this naturalism:

> Life is real! Life is earnest!
>   And the grave is not its goal;
> Dust thou art, to dust returnest,
>   Was not spoken of the soul.

The consummate theologian, the apostle Paul, after admitting his despair, his inability to endure his sufferings to the extent that he "felt the sentence of death," explains that "this happened that we might not rely on ourselves but on God, who raises the dead" (2 Cor. 1:9). In other words, terrible as it is, death is not the victor for the Christian; Christ is the Victor. And because he conquered death, we who rely not on self but on Christ's triumph will finally cheat death and live.

Music and Death

One thing that most young men don't know much about is sickness, suffering, and death. It's older Christians who have experienced these things, and so when great hymn-writers such as Watts and Wesley, Cowper and Newton, Toplady and Palmer, and the rest wrote their poetry, they did so out of a rich and deep maturity of faith under trial. Most young people, however, prefer the superficial, happy-clappy, feel-good outlook expressed in so many contemporary praise songs. Not surprisingly, these are created almost exclusively by young, healthy, and inexperienced Christians.

Thus, we are a generation almost entirely unfamiliar with what Christians for centuries have been singing with the dying. In entertainment music produced by the young and healthy, it is no surprise that the themes of suffering and death are conspicuously missing. Exit these themes in Christian worship, and a vast dark void awaits the young when they are old, the healthy when they are dying. David sang of walking in the valley of the shadow of death, so did Watts, Wesley, Lyte, and Bonar, and so should we, the young with the old, the healthy with the dying.

When I was a child, my father established the tradition of singing around our table. I was young, so I squirmed and fidgeted at times. But now I'm convinced that family singing is one of those celestial joys that God gives his children as a foretaste of heaven, all the more when hovering on the brink.

In my father's final days on this earth, we sang his favorite hymns with him. Moments before he died, choked with emotion, we sang: "The Lord's my Shepherd, I'll not want . . . Yea, though I walk in death's dark vale, Yet will I fear none ill, For thou art with me." When he was suffering and morphine brought no relief, it was the Word of God and singing hymns that brought relief and comfort to him and to us. Name the happy-clappy chorus that is up to this. More than once my father joined in when we least expected it, his eyes brightening as he harmonized on the bass line.

Through the sanctified habits of my father's methodical Christian life, God granted us strength as we sang together, "Whate'er my God ordains is right, his Holy will abideth." Or "Strength I find to meet my trials here." Or "Stayed upon Jehovah, hearts are fully blest, finding, as he promised, perfect peace and rest." Singing these manly, psalm-like words together did not make us stoics; we were often choked with emotion. But it did turn our trembling hearts from fear to faith.

Gaining "a heart of wisdom" this way is not easy. But only when you acknowledge the delusion of eternal youth and own up to the fact that your days on this earth are few will a young man find daily satisfaction in Christ's love. Real men will number their days aright. Then and only then can you "sing for joy and be glad all [your] days" (Ps. 90:14).

Prayer Resolves

- To remind myself often of the shortness of my days
- To seek wisdom before temporal pleasures
- To look to Christ to "establish the work of [my] hands" (Ps. 90:17)
- To meditate more on the eternality of God and his ordering the days of my life in the world
- To love and appreciate my dad and find joy and gladness with him while we live

Scripture Memory

"Teach us to number our days aright, that we may gain a heart of wisdom."

Psalm 90:12

For Discussion

1. How has your father had to face the reality of his growing older and eventually dying?
2. What does it mean when the psalmist asked the Lord to "establish the work of our hands"?
3. What work has God called you and your father to accomplish for him during the overlapping years of your lives?
4. What steps should you be taking to be about that work now?

"O God, Our Help in Ages Past"

Time, like an ever-rolling stream,
Bears all her sons away.
They fly forgotten as a dream
Flies at the op'ning day.

Isaac Watts, 1719

For Further Study

Read and discuss Psalm 103; Ecclesiastes 12; Isaiah 40

18

LIFE AND DEATH

Genesis 18:25

For some, the delusion of eternal youth gets tragically shattered. In the mystery of God's providence, some fathers have to go through the deep waters of laying a dear son in the grave. None of us knows whether we will be that son, or that father. My friend, sailing companion, and teaching colleague at Covenant High School, Ralph McLin, is one of those fathers whom God ordained to find grace to help in the deepest, darkest tragedy any parent can envision. Perhaps there is special divine grace to be found in such a trial. Our heavenly Father can comfort like no other because he, too, is a father who endured the death of his beloved Son.

Without Warning

I had climbed this mountain with my son once before. That time, we had come off late and collapsed gratefully into the truck at the trailhead, anticipating that hot shower and meal at home—only to find that the truck battery was dead. The ten-mile slog in the dark from the trailhead down the mountain to a phone was exhausting, but somehow it had been right. Joel and I had talked, listened to the owls hooting in the rain forest, and shared in our fatigue.

This time, it didn't feel right. In fact, it felt all wrong. As my truck's headlights picked out the little white Toyota sedan parked by itself at the trailhead—cold, empty, alone in the gathering darkness—we *knew* it was wrong. Joel never came home late from a climb without notifying us. He was long overdue. Worried, his mother and I had set out from home after supper up to the Mount Washington trailhead in the Olympic National Forest.

Home just one day after his junior year at Wheaton College, Joel was reveling in getting some "serious altitude" in the mountains he loved. It was typical of Joel to go off by himself and have his private time with God. He was a kid who went deeper into the woods and higher on the mountain than most of us.

Now, as we scanned the high snowfields glowing eerily white among the black crags, we strained our eyes for any sign of movement. We called Joel's name and honked the truck horn repeatedly. Wind and a nearby waterfall mocked our efforts. We pleaded with God to strengthen and uphold our son if he was injured up on the mountain, and guide him down if he was lost. All the while, we expected him to come bursting out of the brush at the trailhead, exclaiming, "Hey, Mom, Dad! What are you doing up here?"

No such surprise occurred. I knew better than to think he might have gotten lost. Joel didn't take wrong turns. From childhood he had demonstrated an uncanny sense of direction. I had done my best to teach Joel and his older brother Matt to glance back regularly when climbing so that a particular landmark, such as a gnarled tree or an unusual boulder, could be recognized on the way back down. Over the years Joel had honed his skills, learning to read the lay of the land, the pitch and angle of rock or snow, and could pick the best route through rock or glacier.

Previously on Mount Rainier

I remember, two summers before, feeling fully confident in Joel's abilities as he led our team up Mount Rainier. On that trip, as we crested Disappointment Cleaver, we passed teams that had jumped out ahead of us, one waiting for airlift from a chopper struggling to reach them at the twelve-thousand-foot elevation. Soberly our team passed the mummy-bagged body of a climber on a mountain-rescue litter, a man about my age who had suffered a fatal heart attack while climbing with his daughter on his birthday. Shaking off the implications of that vision and focusing on my breathing, I followed while Joel led the rope on toward the summit.

As the wind increased, our progress slowed. To hang on to the mountain, we drove our axes deeper into the ice and hunkered down more and more with each step. Joel stopped at about 13,500 feet and waited for the three of us to catch up. He had noticed that fresh snow from the previous night was still driven unbroken across the route, meaning we were the only climbers that high on Rainier, with no one ahead of us and no one coming on up from below. No backup. No radio. A decision must be made. Close as we were, in these conditions we were still an hour from the summit, with clouds lowering. We felt strong, but Joel, even in his prime and wanting that first summit of Rainier so badly that he could taste it, suggested the wise thing—turn back. We did.

Call for Help

Now, as Kathryn and I furtively scanned the silhouetted ridge, we knew we had to do the wise thing. We called for help. Phone coverage was spotty, but we contacted our neighbors, who relayed the message to others.

Within an hour, Kathryn's brother Don arrived with flashlights and radios. He and I decided to begin searching. By this time it was fully dark, and using my best memory of my previous climb with Joel, we found the unmarked trail and began climbing.

The vestige of a trail soon changed to a faint boot track and then became snowbank and rock. The wind blew my repeated calls back into my face, and my prayers were that God might simply help us find him, and ease his suffering if he were injured.

Meanwhile, the sheriff had arrived, and was communicating with us on the two-way radio from the truck where Kathryn waited. They could see us wave our flashlights and encouraged us to keep on going.

Leaving Don, who didn't have proper footwear, I climbed ahead in the faint moonlight, scrambling up over rocky outcroppings, until I reached a cliff that I knew I could not negotiate.

I had failed to find Joel. I could do no more. With a heavy heart, I picked my way back down to Don, and we headed down into a canyon, thinking that Joel might have come back that way. Perhaps we could find tracks. There were none. Bone-weary, we finally arrived back at the truck at dawn. The sheriff had called Olympic Mountain Rescue (OMR), as well as a helicopter, on its way from Fort Lewis.

As Mason County Search and Rescue (MCSR) began to set up their base station, we heard the chopper coming up the canyon below. It was equipped with heat-sensing radar that would detect Joel if he were visible anywhere from the air. But our hopes were dashed when the helicopter had to turn back because of high winds on the summit ridge.

A growing fear gnawed around the edges of my native optimism, and I pushed it back again and again as Kathryn and I waited through the long morning and into the afternoon while OMR made its painstakingly slow preparations for ground search.

The MCSR team of young people, some of whom knew Joel, could be heard working their way up a distant ridge shouting in unison, "Joel! Joel!" With every new effort our hopes surged, but then receded like a retreating wave on the sand.

I wanted desperately to go with the climbers on their search, but they refused to allow it. They knew I was already exhausted after my nighttime efforts and didn't want two rescues on their hands.

At last they were on their way up, and we listened in when we could to radio transmissions as they searched. "We think we've picked up the trail" came the thin, crackly voice on the base radio. "Yes!" I shouted in my mind. "Now we have a chance!"

Meanwhile, another chopper could be heard clacking and thumping its way up from below. It landed in the small wide spot in the fork of the main road and the Mount Ellinore spur, awash in wind and dust. A group of jumpsuit-clad searchers climbed out and were briefed by the sheriff at the base station.

They established contact with the climbers. We waited for what seemed like an eternity to hear whether they were successful. The day was waning, and a decision had to be made soon or there would not be enough time to complete the search before nightfall.

The cold fingers of fear and doubt tightened ever so surely around our hearts as we realized that this was the last chance. Finally we deciphered the message that the searchers had traced Joel's steps through the snow up to a steep cliff where they disappeared, just below the summit ridge. They decided not to follow his apparent route straight up the rock, but went back down and around the base of the rock to another gap where they could see over to the other side of the ridge of rocky cliffs.

They couldn't see Joel but called for an air search of the back side of the ridge to see the areas they couldn't reach in the dwindling daylight. The helicopter roared to life and lifted off, with a pair of searchers sitting on the floor with their legs hanging out of the open cargo doors on each side.

Our hearts leaped again with the strand of hope that they could spot him, and that our Joel would be waving at them from below, waiting for rescue, with some hindering but not life-threatening injury.

I struggled to keep that image alive in my mind as I peered intently through a spotting scope at the upper snow and rocks. At one point I honestly thought I saw a dark form on the snow waving, and for an instant I was almost sick with relief. But another pair of eyes verified that it was just a half-buried treetop swaying in the wind.

My mind was beginning to play the cruel jokes on me that so many others had experienced before. It drained my shallow reserves of energy and hope even further.

The sound of the chopper hacking the thin air around the mountain strengthened, faded, and then increased again. I wasn't sure I wanted to hear anything from the rescuers. I wasn't prepared for the worst, and still couldn't bring my mind to imagine it. Then the word came.

Word at Last

"They've spotted him!" And the final surge of hope rushed through my mind. But I couldn't bring myself to ask the only question left to ask: "Is he still alive?"

Time stood still as we watched a group of rescuers walk toward us. They closed the distance between our truck and the base station with deathly steadiness. The sheriff spoke first.

"They found him," he said. "He is not alive."

His words hit like a sledgehammer. I pressed him: "Are you sure? Could there be a mistake?"

He looked us in the eyes and slowly shook his head. "No, there's no mistake. The crew is retrieving him from the base of the cliff—where he fell."

As the reality of what we were hearing punched its way through the barriers of hope and prayer that we had erected over the last twenty hours, Kathryn and I collapsed to our knees sobbing.

"Oh, no! Oh, God, no! Not our precious Joel! No, God, no! How will we make it without Joel?" It was all so strange, so unthinkable.

The hours that followed left their memories etched in our stunned and aching hearts. Seeing our Joel in the coroner's van and holding his ice-cold hands. Somehow getting off the mountain in a relative's car. That first agonizing night at home. The flood of friends and family enveloping us in love and tears and prayer. The surreal decisions to be made—picking a gravesite, choosing a casket, planning the funeral service. All these decisions seemed at once important and desperately trivial. Joel was gone and was not coming back. Why? What had gone wrong?

Some Tough Questions

Fathers who are reading this, if, in God's all-wise providence, you are called to bear the loss of a child of your own, are you prepared? I am not talking about somehow steeling yourself against the shock and the grief and awful sense of the finality of death, but are you prepared to think about it correctly? I wasn't.

In the midst of the agony of the *why*s were those thoughts and doubts that continually rose to the surface and shouted to be answered in some way.

Where were you, God? Didn't you promise to keep his foot from slipping, to keep your angels in charge over him?

I struggled hard with this. I believed in God's protection of believers. I believed in guardian angels. Only through beginning to understand God's sovereignty did I realize that God had been protecting and upholding Joel in the hour of his death as throughout his life. God hadn't turned his back; he was as much there at that instant as he had ever been.

Was this Joel's fault? Had he made a poor choice to climb that route that day and simply fallen victim to the laws of physics and gravity? This is a tough one, suggested by many well-meaning people. Certainly God didn't push him off that rock. The laws of friction, balance, inertia, and gravity were all in play.

We all make choices in life: what to eat, what to wear, which car to drive, what route to climb. Joel, as all of us do, made his choices—choices that can carry serious consequences. But in struggling with this question I began to realize that no aspect of what happened had taken God by surprise. Joel's steps had been ordered by the Lord. Not by chance, not by physics, not by blind fate, but by the Lord.

In *One Minute After You Die*, Erwin Lutzer says, "Car accidents, heart attacks, cancer—all of these are the means used to open the door of heaven to the children of God. The immediate cause of our death is neither haphazard nor arbitrary."

Was it our fault? Couldn't we have prevented this? As Joel's parents, we wondered whether there was something we should have done to stop this from happening. Had we failed to protect our son? And yet as God continued to reveal the truth of his sovereignty to us, we were humbled and corrected. We had had nothing to do with it. Joel's death was out of our hands. It was God's work.

Understanding that truth has been the antidote to the poison of guilt over the loss of Joel. We yield to God's good, sovereign will. And in that acquiescence is peace and healing. Abraham acknowledged, "Will not the Judge of all the earth do right?" (Gen. 18:25).

Similarly, Samuel Rutherford encouraged Mistress Taylor after the loss of her son:

> The supreme and absolute Former of all things giveth not an account of any of His matters. The good Husbandman may pluck His roses, and gather in His lilies at mid-summer, and He may transplant young trees out of the lower ground to the higher, where they may have more of the sun, and a more free air, at any season of the year. What is that to you or me? The goods are His own. The Creator of time and winds did a merciful injury to nature, in landing the passenger so early.

God's Mysterious Plan

How should you think about your future? That time when you will finally be prepared physically, academically, spiritually to serve the Lord? Is it an end point that beckons from afar, glimmering off in the distance like a mirage? After high school? After college? After marriage? After financial success?

Think again, and recognize God as he really is: sovereign. He alone knows your future. Your future is not something that merely unfolds as you make life decisions. Pain or loss, or early death, God graciously planned every detail before you were a twinkle in your parents' eyes.

A. W. Tozer writes to young men like you:

To the child of God there is no such thing as an accident. He travels an appointed way. The path he treads was chosen for him when as yet he was not, when as yet he had existence only in the mind of God. Accidents may indeed appear to befall him and misfortune stalk his way; but these evils will be so in appearance only and will seem evils only because we cannot read the secret script of God's hidden providence and so cannot discover the ends at which He aims.

Tozer continues:

The man of true faith may live in the absolute assurance that his steps are ordered by the Lord. For him, misfortune is outside the bounds of possibility. He cannot be torn from this earth one hour ahead of the time which God has appointed, and he cannot be detained on earth one moment after God is done with him here.

Live for God

Face it. God's sovereignty ultimately trumps your plans, as bright and exciting as they may be. So why plan and prepare for your future? Because God's ends are found smack-dab in the middle of that very process! He isn't waiting for you to get ready to be his or standing by while you prepare to serve him someday. He is working right now. In the present.

What he wants to do with you, young man, he is doing right now. The life you live every day is his workshop. It's not just about the end result, as great as that can certainly be, but about the process of that work in your life day by day.

My son Joel had plans. He wanted to serve God, too. He was getting ready: going to Wheaton, in ROTC, taking Bible classes and voice lessons, leading kids on wilderness trips. And in it all, he was serving God.

Joel, like you, only dimly realized the impact he was having on the people around him. Every kind word, every encouragement of friend or family, every act of courage and leadership, every letter written, every shout of victory from a mountaintop, every Burger King meal given up to a homeless man—these, for Joel, were the present and the future. They were all that would be.

Ponder this well. Does God have a long life planned for you? You do not know. In an instant, like my Joel's, your life could end. Job said, "I know that thou wilt bring me to death, and to the house appointed for all living" (Job 30:23 KJV). And because of the shortness of life, the wise man wrote to young men, "Remember your Creator in the days of your youth" (Eccl. 12:1).

The days of your youth may be the only days you will have. Either way, serve God in the present. Love and honor your father and mother. Make the most of every opportunity, of every conversation. Live to the hilt now for God's glory, and all will be well when God calls you to himself.

Prayer Resolves

- To make the most of our time together as father and son
- To keep our eyes on Christ and heaven while enjoying life in this world

Scripture Memory

"Even though I walk through the valley of the shadow of death, I will fear no evil, for you are with me; your rod and your staff, they comfort me."

Psalm 23:4

For Discussion

1. When children get hurt or killed, where were their guardian angels?
2. What is the place of vigorous outdoor activities for fathers and sons?
3. How can fathers and sons spend more meaningful time together?

4. How can you live today so that you or your father will find
   hope when God takes one of you away in death?

"Higher Ground"

I'm pressing on the upward way,
New heights I'm gaining every day;
Still praying as I'm onward bound,
"Lord, plant my feet on higher ground."

Johnson Oatman Jr., 1898

For Further Study

Read and discuss *The Happy Mountaineer*, by Amy Carmichael; *Saints'
Everlasting Rest*, by Richard Baxter

19

TO CURSE OR NOT TO CURSE?

Job 1:1–2:10

Curse God and Die

It was November 29, 1917, Jack's nineteenth birthday. It was also his first day of trench warfare. Some birthday party! Later he wrote about that day: "The first bullet I heard 'whined' like a journalist's or a peacetime poet's bullet. At that moment there was something not exactly like fear . . . a little quavering signal that said, 'This is War. This is what Homer wrote about.' "

One day he had been a fresh young college student; now he was a soldier. After a hasty few months of training, he was dubbed a second lieutenant in the Somerset Light Infantry and shipped off to France. Near Arras he heard that first of many bullets. When not dodging those bullets, he wrote down reflections on his experience.

The war—the frights, the cold, the smell, the horribly smashed men still moving like half-crushed beetles, the sitting or standing corpses, the landscape of sheer earth without blade of grass, the boots worn day and night till they seemed to grow to your feet . . . I have gone to sleep marching and woken again and found myself marching still. Familiarity both with the very old and the very recent dead . . . I came to know, and pity, and reverence the ordinary man.

In April 1918 at Mount Bernenchon, near Lillers, France, an artillery shell whistled louder and closer than the rest. Then it hit. Erupting in a deafening explosion, the shrapnel instantly killed Jack's friend, who had been a father figure to him. And it hit Jack. He wrote, "The moment just after I had been hit . . . I found that I was not breathing and concluded that this was death." Perhaps at the field hospital at Etaples, perhaps at a convalescent camp on the Salisbury Plain, embittered by his experience, Jack began writing a poem:

Come, let us curse our Master ere we die,
For all our hopes in endless ruin lie.
The good is dead. Let us curse God most High.

Laugh then and slay. Shatter all things of worth,
Heap torment still on torment for thy mirth—
Thou art not Lord while there are Men on earth.

Jack was his nickname. His real name was Clive Staples Lewis. The lines above appeared in his first book, *Spirits in Bondage*, a collection of poems that Lewis wrote while a young atheist and that he described to a friend as "mainly strung around the idea that nature is diabolical and malevolent and that God, if he exists, is outside of and in opposition to the cosmic arrangements."

Perhaps, considering the horrors of World War I that Lewis suffered, his bitterness and cynicism are more understandable. There were horrors aplenty. On the first day alone of the Battle of the Somme, the lives of twenty thousand young men were cut short, many of them so mangled by artillery shells, by the tramping feet of advancing and retreating soldiers, by the debris, mud, and carnage, that in the five-month battle more than fifty thousand soldiers' bodies were so obliterated that they have no known graves. From 1914 to 1918, an average of fifty-six hundred young men died each day of those five years, more than ten million lives. No wonder Lewis penned the cynical lines "laugh then and slay."

God Gives; God Takes Away

You are young and probably in reasonably good health. Some of you are athletes. You run fast. You hit hard, throw hard, play hard. You feel the power of your muscles, and you're thrilled by it all. Enjoy it. But know this: you won't always have it.

Similarly, Job had everything going for him; he was a great man. God said of him, "There is no one on earth like him" (Job 1:8). He was wealthy. He had a good family. He had the respect of his peers. Most of all, he was upright and blameless, fearing God and turning away from evil.

Then it hit. First his oxen and donkeys were stolen; then fire fell from heaven and consumed his sheep and servants. With that news still ringing in his ears, Job learned from another of his servants that all his camels had been carried off and that the servants responsible to care for them had been put to the sword. With no time to recover, Job then listened as another messenger reported the most dreaded of all news: the house had collapsed on his children. "They are dead."

This was cosmic devastation of the highest order. In one day Job lost everything, including his children. In one fell swoop, he went from prosperous and content to destitute and barren. What would you do? What did Job do? "He fell to the ground in worship and said: 'Naked I came from my mother's womb, and naked I will depart. The LORD gave and the LORD has taken away; may the name of the LORD be praised' " (1:21).

What Job did not know was the divine perspective. He hadn't heard God initiate it all by saying to Satan, "Have you considered my servant

217

Job? There is no one on earth like him; he is blameless and upright, a man who fears God and shuns evil" (1:8). But it wasn't over yet.

The crowning blow would touch Job's own body, now covered with "painful sores from the soles of his feet to the top of his head" (2:7). Worse still, his wife took one look at him and said, "Curse God and die!" (2:9). Young, wounded, and bitter, C. S. Lewis would have agreed. But not Job. "Shall we accept good from God," he replied, "and not trouble?" (2:10).

Cosmic Tournament?

Satan, "the accuser of the brethren," steps up and accuses Job of fearing God for selfish reasons, as *quid pro quo*—a mere economic arrangement. The fiend assumes that Job has faith in God only because of all the material blessings God has given him. In short, he says: Remove the hedge around Job and all your blessings on him, take away his stuff, and "he will surely curse you to your face" (Job 2:5).

Satan has thrown down the cosmic gauntlet. Here is the big question set up and worked out throughout the book: Is Satan right, or is God? Is Job "blameless" because of material blessings and health? Will Job curse God when good things are taken away? These questions drive the drama of the story forward, keep us on the edge of our seats, and compel us to read on, to find out who is right about Job: God or Satan.

This is high-stakes drama, just like your life and mine. Here the narrator lays out the real "war to end all wars." Put yourself in Job's place. Okay, you're not blameless, but to the extent to which your life is lived as a Christian, why do you do it? Why do you claim to be a Christian? Why do you, more or less, refrain from sin? Satan wants to ruin you. He wants your spiritual hide. What will it take to make you "curse God and die"?

So far, Job "did not sin by charging God with wrongdoing" (1:22), but the inspired anonymous narrator hints at the sin that will creep in on Job as his trial grinds on. So far, "Job did not sin in what he said"

(2:10b) . . . so far. But Job is hurting; he's in anguish. Chapter 3 gets closer. It opens with cursing: "Job open[s] his mouth and curse[s] the day of his birth." In expansive, ancient Near Eastern eloquence, did Job ever curse! But he did not curse God, as Satan was so confident he would. Still, poor Job fears his "turmoil" might mean that in the end he is one of the wicked, and righteous Job would rather not have been born than be one of the wicked. Satan loses round one.

Some Friends!

Satan is the great accuser, and as if Satan were now "roaming through the earth" (1:7; 2:2) in the shape of three friends, Job's comforters begin their accusations. Eliphaz (descendant of Esau; see Gen. 36) leads off, patronizing Job and accusing him of impatience—ironic, considering that Job is remembered for patience. "Should not your piety be your confidence and your blameless ways your hope?" (4:6). Job's reputation preceded him. God had declared Job "blameless" (1:8) at the outset of the drama. All-wise Eliphaz doubts it and rails on: "Where were the upright ever destroyed?" (4:7). Curious, isn't it? God had also declared Job "upright." And just as God had said to Satan, "Have you considered my servant Job?" (1:8; 2:3). Eliphaz attempts to ape the divine perspective: "Consider now: Who, being innocent, has ever perished?" (4:7). He goes on to claim that he has these deep insights into the cause of Job's distress because "a word was secretly brought to me, . . . a spirit glided past" (4:12, 15). Some comforter! Here is a "friend" who presumes to speak for God, to have a corner on the divine perspective on Job's trial, and for all that, makes Job's trial far worse. Don't be like friend Eliphaz!

And don't be like friend Bildad! Not only does he doubt that Job is "blameless and upright" (1:8; 2:3), as God declared him, but he presumes to know why Job's children were swept away: "When your children sinned against [God], he gave them over to the penalty of their sin" (8:4). Some comfort! Who is this guy, that he presumes to know the hearts of Job and his children—and the mind of God?

And don't be like friend Zophar, either. He's so convinced that Job is getting what he deserves for some specific, hidden sin that he tells Job, "God has even forgotten some of your sin" (11:6b).

Predictably, Job takes no comfort from their words, and exposes the problem with their brand of comfort: "Men at ease have contempt for misfortune" (12:5), and "A despairing man should have the devotion of his friends" (6:14).

Arrows of the Almighty

Like most trials, Job's grinds on, and as it does, Job draws ever closer to "charging God with wrongdoing" (1:22). He knows God is absolutely sovereign, that God is the First Cause, the One who gives and the One who takes. Job calls his troubles "God's terrors" (6:4), and says that God has "devastated my entire household. You have bound me . . . God assails me" (16:7–9). Not once does he stoop to giving Satan credit for all that has come upon him. "The hand of the LORD has done this" (12:9), Job states as an irrefutable theological fact. No one could ever charge God with wrongdoing unless he believed that God was the One doing things. If God were not sovereign, it would never occur to Job to charge God with wrongdoing. But one hears a hint of accusation in his words. Though Job clearly knows that God is great, he seems now to wonder whether God is good.

Now in anguish, confusion, and despair, Job gives "free rein to [his] complaint" (10:1). He begins to see God not as his friend but as his opponent, the "watcher of men" (7:20) who stalks Job to crush him for his sport, to "laugh then and slay," as Lewis put it in his pre-Christian poem. Job declares his innocence: "I am blameless" (9:21), he cries, and then begins a defense of his self-righteousness. He is no idolater, no oppressor of the poor, no lover of riches, no womanizer: "I made a covenant with my eyes not to look lustfully at a girl" (31:1). Note how much better these qualities sounded when God said them about Job than when Job says them about himself. Nevertheless, Job's conscience is clear, and his friends' accusations have made him desperate to clear himself.

In that desperation he turns things around. He implores God to "turn away from me so I can have a moment's joy" (10:20). Unlike the psalmist (Ps. 16:11), Job is losing his grip on the fact that only in the presence of God does the Christian find "fullness of joy " (Ps. 16:11 ESV) no matter how great seem the "slings and arrows of outrageous fortune," as Shakespeare's Hamlet bemoaned.

Rage and Praise

Once you and I get things turned around, it's hard to get out of the knot. So now with Job. Weary of arguing with his foolish friends, and emboldened by despair, he said, "I desire to speak to the Almighty and to argue my case with God" (Job 13:3). From our comfortable vantage point, this seems too bold, almost arrogant. And so it is, but convinced of his own righteousness and of God's wrongdoing, Job has things desperately reversed.

Yet in the midst of this confusion are moments when Job sees with remarkable clarity. At those times we are witness to some of the most eloquent echoes of his original response of worship and confidence in God. "Though he slay me, yet will I hope in him," exclaims Job (13:15). Later he says, "Even now my witness is in heaven; my advocate is on high" (16:19).

When held in tension with his great suffering, these declarations of blameless Job's faith are splendid beyond words. For a brief moment at the center of the book, anguished Job looks heavenward and offers this primal confession: "I know that my Redeemer lives, and that in the end he will stand upon the earth. And after my skin has been destroyed, yet in my flesh I will see God; I myself will see him with my own eyes—I, and not another. How my heart yearns within me!" (19:25–27). Little wonder such grand and fitting music flowed from George Frederick Handel's pen in 1741, as he meditated on these words. For an instant, all Job's raging melts away in this high confessional praise.

But it lasts only a moment; the clouds lower, and the raging resumes. "I will surely defend my ways to his face," says Job (13:15).

In his frustration, he proceeds to demand of his Redeemer, "Let me speak, and you reply" (13:22b). Then follows a barrage of accusation and self-justification: "God has wronged me!" (19:6). "God . . . has denied me justice" (27:2). "I will maintain my righteousness" (27:6). And in a final salvo of rage he declares: "I sign now my defense—let the Almighty answer me" (31:35).

Whew! These are strong words, close to blasphemous ones. Think about it. Ascribing wrongdoing to a thrice-holy God. Maintaining one's own righteousness and demanding that the Almighty take that, and answer the charges you have laid before him. I'm reminded of another stanza from bruised atheist C. S. Lewis's pen after the crushing ugliness of World War I:

> Yet I will not bow down to thee nor love thee,
> For looking in my own heart I can prove thee,
> And know this frail bruised being is above thee.

Yikes! In these lines, Lewis expresses his mistaken and baldly arrogant sense that his ways are better than God's ways; that he has God figured out, and he doesn't like what he's figured out; that therefore, he refuses to bow down or love God. Wise, mature, Christian Lewis, many years later, described one of the demon's favorite and most effective temptations: "Make the patient a critic where he ought to be a pupil."

When Job charges God with wrongdoing, however, is he cursing like Lewis? Being a critic, yes; sinning, yes; but cursing? I don't think so. If he were, Satan would now have won and the book would be concluded.

Which it is not. There is more to be said on God's behalf, more than Job realizes at this point. God will finally enter the scene and speak directly with Job—school him, as it were. And Job will stop being a critic and become a humble pupil, one who bows down to the Almighty and loves him. Whatever else he does not understand—and there is a great deal Job will not understand—he will know that he has been loved by the Almighty through all his troubles.

Prayer Resolves

- To learn when to be silent in affliction
- To learn to wait on the Lord in troubles
- To replace argument and complaint with humble praise and adoration

Scripture Memory

"Who can speak and have it happen if the Lord has not decreed it? Is it not from the mouth of the Most High that both calamities and good things come? Why should any living man complain when punished for his sins?"

Lamentations 3:37–39

For Discussion

1. Is it possible for you to be confused and doubting and yet not sinning?
2. Based on the errors of Job's "miserable comforters," how should you comfort someone who is afflicted?
3. Discuss the trials of someone you know and love. How has this person been patient in those afflictions? Plan specific ways in which you will bring comfort to him or her.

"God Moves in a Mysterious Way"

God moves in a mysterious way,
His wonders to perform.
He plants his footsteps in the sea
And rides upon the storm.

William Cowper, 1774

For Further Study

Job 19

20

HAND-ON- MOUTH WORSHIP

Job 40–42

Young Wisdom

Who can see the Lord's face and live? Satan had predicted that if Job did see God's face, it would be to curse him. After the initial blows of the Almighty, Job instead fell on his face in worship. Now Job demands an audience to "defend my ways to [God's] face" (Job 13:15). Like few men in the history of the world, Job will, in fact, be given a face-to-face audience with God. But not yet.

To everyone's relief, Job's three friends finally stop accusing. Then Job lays out his own righteousness as his defense. Next, young, wise Elihu reluctantly speaks, offering a defense of his youthful wisdom. Isn't this like God? He delights to show his wisdom through the unexpected. Abel was the younger brother, so was Isaac, so was Jacob, and so was Joseph. Jesus confounded the elders in the synagogue when he was twelve, and Paul urged Timothy to not let others despise him for his youth. So it is in God's economy. Take heart, young man, and be wise early, like Elihu.

After rebuking the friends for not proving Job wrong, Elihu then proceeds to instruct Job, but not as the foolish friends had done. "You are not right," said Elihu to Job, "for God is greater than man. Why do you complain to him that he answers none of man's words? For God does speak—now one way, now another—though man may not perceive it" (33:12–14).

Elihu proceeds to show Job that his righteousness is a result of grace; that Job, like all mankind, is a sinner, and great though his troubles are, Job has not gotten the full force of what he deserved from God's hand; that his righteousness is a result of redemption (33:27).

From here, Elihu proceeds to dismantle Job's argument, especially his accusation that God had denied him justice (34:5–29). "It is unthinkable that God would do wrong, that the Almighty would pervert justice" (v. 12). God is the great Originator of everything, including justice. Justice is not outside of God, something he must keep in mind and submit to; it is an intrinsic attribute of God himself. That is why Elihu tells Job that it is unthinkable for God to do wrong, to be unjust. "Will you condemn the just and mighty One?" (v. 17) he implores Job. "Should God then reward you on your terms . . . ?" (v. 33). As if to say, this sovereign God, who rules over men, nations, and all creation—is he subject to any of your terms, Job?

Next, Elihu rebukes Job for rebellion, for speaking to and about God "like a wicked man" (34:36). He then shows Job how insignificant his sinning or his doing right is, how independent God is from Job, how God's will, ways, justice—every dimension of his being—is independent of anything that Job does or doesn't do. From there Elihu ascribes "justice to [his] Maker" (36:3), and he ascribes arrogance to Job for arguing with God (36:8–9).

Then Elihu warns Job: "Beware of turning to evil, which you seem to prefer to affliction" (36:21), a wise caution for a young man to remember when perplexed by suffering. "God is exalted in his power," he continued. "Who is a teacher like him?" (36:22). And as this wise young man tries to help Job see more of the wonder of God's power and sovereignty in creation, he finds himself overcome with joy: "At this my heart pounds and leaps from its place" (37:1).

At last, Elihu makes a statement that is little short of a microcosm of the meaning of the entire book of Job: "God's voice thunders in marvelous ways; he does great things beyond our understanding" (37:5). Or, put another way, "The Almighty is beyond our reach and exalted in power; in his justice and great righteousness, he does not oppress" (37:23). God is beyond the reach of any of us; his ways are higher than our ways. Blameless Job needed to grow in his understanding of this—and so do you.

"Before Your Face Questions Die Away"

In C. S. Lewis's arguably most enigmatic book, *Till We Have Faces*, Lewis created a troubled and beleaguered protagonist who, like Job, had to undergo some pretty tough trials before finding peace and rest. Like Job, Lewis's ugly barbarian queen, Orual, complained in bitterness of soul at the gods and accused them of dealing falsely with her. "It was of course the gods' old trick; blow the bubble up big before you prick it." As in Lewis's World War I poetry, Orual believed "there is no creature (toad, scorpion, or serpent) so noxious to man as the gods." Unlike Job, however, Lewis's queen did curse God. Or did she? Maybe it was only her flawed conception of the gods that she was cursing.

As Lewis brings the tale to its grand, confessional climax, the troubled queen found herself making a full disclosure, voicing her complaint from the center of her soul. In this full disclosure of her soul's bitterness and despair, she made a discovery, not unlike the one that Job is about to make: "I saw well why the gods do not speak to us openly, nor let us answer. Till that word can be dug out of us, why should they hear the babble that we think we mean? How can they meet us face to face till we have faces?"

Lewis's queen came to understand that she could never have a face-to-face encounter with God until she had her own face, that is, until she saw herself in her true features, till she saw how ugly she was, till she acknowledged that it was her soul that was ugly, not simply her face. Her anger at the gods for giving no answer to her complaint melted away in her final confession: "You are yourself the answer. Before your face questions die away."

This will be Job. Yes, he has done a good deal of babbling about how ill-used he's been by God, how unjustly and unfairly God has dealt with him. But now God is about to speak to Job—face-to-face. Such a divine encounter will strip Job of the last of everything he thinks he possesses—and it will graciously restore everything to Job. Such is the expansive mercy of God to his children.

God Speaks

Just as Elihu had said, "God's voice thunders in marvelous ways" (37:5), now the Almighty's voice really does thunder as he answers Job out of the storm: "Who is this that darkens my counsel with words without knowledge?" (38:2).

When his trial first came upon him, Job "did not sin in what he said" (2:10), but now God goes right to the issue of Job's words— words of argument and complaint, sinful words that even accused God of wrongdoing. "Brace yourself like a man; I will question you, and you shall answer me" (38:3).

Job had things switched around. It's God who asks the questions, not Job. "Out of the storm" (38:1), the Lord proceeds to pose a series of questions calculated to show Job the true nature of God's power and sovereignty and goodness in his dealing with men and beasts in his world. "Where were you when I laid the earth's foundation? Tell me, if you understand" (38:4).

At last Job has gotten what he longed for: a face-to-face encounter with the sovereign Ruler of all things. How many men get that? Job longed for conversation with his intimate friend, with his God, and now he has it. What Job has been demanding, he gets: God does answer him (38:1). But not quite in the way Job wanted. Only the deepest, most intimate friendships can sustain satire.

In this encounter, God brings to light Job's sinful words by employing a long string of satirical questions that gently, almost humorously, ridicule Job's mistaken ideas about God's ways. "Do you send the lightning bolts on their way?" God asks Job. "Do they report to you, 'Here we are'?" (v. 35). I'm sure that godly Job blushed and diverted his eyes at God's jest. And though God says all this out of the storm, he doesn't speak to crush Job. God wants this frail, bruised man to know more of God's splendor and power, his unimpeachable sovereignty, his perfect justice, his expansive love, and his providential care for all things—including Job himself.

Satan had accused Job; Job's friends had accused Job; Job had accused God; Elihu had accused the three friends and Job; now God accuses Job. "Will the one who contends with the Almighty correct him? Let him who accuses God answer him!" (40:2).

Just as the psalmist in Psalm 73 enters the sanctuary, the very presence of God, and finally sees things aright, when Job meets with God, when God speaks with him face-to-face, far from cursing as Satan had predicted, Job responds with self-abasement: "I am unworthy—how can I reply to you? I put my hand over my mouth. I spoke once, but I have no answer—twice, but I will say no more" (40:4–5). Just as Job's comforters were at their best when they were silent, so now Job learns to "do everything without complaining or arguing" (Phil. 2:14). It sounds almost too simple. But there it is. Authentic and legitimate as doubt and confusion are, when they grow into unconstrained complaint and argument, they cease to be virtues and must be rooted out, confessed, and forsaken, as upright Job is learning.

But God is not finished with Job's tutorial, and when he says the same thing twice, we do well to sit up and listen. "Brace yourself like a man; I will question you, and you shall answer me" (40:7). Here is the proper order: God's asking you hard questions rather than your presuming to ask him.

"Would you discredit my justice?" God demands. "Would you condemn me to justify yourself" (40:8)? "Do you have an arm like God's, and can your voice thunder like his? Then adorn yourself with glory and splendor" (40:9–10). Okay, Job, if you think you are God, prove it! And then God declares the sin that sprang up for Job while he was perplexed over his suffering. If you can be God and do all these things that I do, if you can "look at every proud man and humble him, . . . then I myself will admit to you that your own right hand can save you" (40:12–14). Job's anguish over his affliction unearthed a self-righteous man who thought more of his goodness than he did of grace and his need for redemption. Sound familiar? Look in the mirror.

God proceeds to show Job not only how much greater divine power is than the most powerful creatures God made and commands, in marvelous descriptions of animals, from storks to behemoth, but he also shows Job that if he cares for and provides for the likes of ostriches, how much more does he care for and love Job!

Like the loving heavenly Father that he is, God reprimands his son. Remember that Job had cursed the day of his birth and bemoaned that he was not carried from the womb to his tomb? As if gently reminding Job of this cursing, God asks him, "Who shut up the sea behind doors when it burst forth from the womb[?] . . . From whose womb comes the ice? Who gave birth to the frost?" (38:8, 29). Then in chapter 39: "Do you know when the mountain goats give birth? Do you watch when the doe bears her fawn? Do you count the months till they bear? Do you know the time they give birth?" (39:1–2). The point is subtle but poignant. Job's life—your life—is absolutely in God's hands, in every detail, from its beginning to its end. Thus, there is no place for cursing when God is the sovereign of life.

Then God proceeds to show Job how powerless he is next to one of God's most powerful creatures, the fire-breathing Leviathan. If Job is powerless to make a pet out of the mighty Leviathan, to "put him on a leash" (41:5), how can Job presume to stand against God? The suggestion is profound and unmistakable: Job cannot presume to make a pet out of his God, to hold God in his hand. "Everything under heaven," declares God, "belongs to me" (41:11). In short, God speaks to help Job see just how small he is compared to the God who made and rules all creation. Likewise, a wise young man must know just how small he is.

God Is Always Right

After all this, Job removes his hand from his mouth and speaks aright: "I know that you can do all things; no plan of yours can be thwarted" (42:2). Why does Job say this? Because here is the confessional correction to all of Job's raging, arguing, and complaining against God. Here Job humbly acknowledges the absolute sovereignty of God. And so must you.

Virtually all your spiritual problems stem from attempting to dethrone God and his sovereignty. You want to make a pet of him and lead him about on your chain. You are a powerful young man, after all, and you want to rule the world for yourself, including God. Frankly, he gets in the way of lots of your plans.

Place your hand over your mouth, as upright Job did. Acknowledge with Job that God and his ways are "too wonderful for [you] to know" (42:3). Say with Job: "My ears had heard of you, but now my eyes have seen you. Therefore I despise myself and repent in dust and ashes" (42:5–6).

Does Job repent of some secret wickedness that brought these troubles on him, as his friends kept insisting? Does he repent for cursing God, as Satan insisted? No—blameless Job repents of ascribing, in the depths of his anguish and misery, wrongdoing and injustice to the Almighty. He repents of thinking too highly of his questions and too lowly of God's answers. He repents of trying to justify his ways to God instead of, as John Milton put it, "justify[ing] the ways of God to man." He repents of not continuing to confess that "the LORD gave and the LORD has taken away; may the name of the LORD be praised" (1:21).

Satan lost. Job did not curse God to his face. God was right. God is always right, and that is the message of Job. Remember, Job didn't have Job, the book. You do. Be patient in affliction. Pour your heart out to God in your troubles. Tell him everything: your doubts, your confusions. But don't cross the line into questioning his sovereignty, his justice, his goodness. Come what may—whether God blesses you, afflicts you, or restores you to even greater prominence, as he did Job—God is always sovereign and he is always good in the exercise of his sovereignty. Never doubt it, and you can remain a strong man in affliction.

Satan hates a strong man. Give Satan what he hates. Render to God what he loves: your humble praise, patient obedience, quiet adoration in trouble. Then, when in your "flesh [you] . . . see God" (19:26) face-to-face, as Job did, all the deepest yearnings of your heart will rise up and spill over in deep humility and repentance, and in Handel-like eternal praise. That is what you were made for. Do it now. Do it for eternity.

Prayer Resolves

- To cultivate a deeper sense of the sovereignty of God in all my life
- To cultivate a deeper sense of the goodness of God in all my life
- To replace argument and complaint with humble praise and adoration

Scripture Memory

"I know that my Redeemer lives, and that in the end he will stand upon the earth. And after my skin has been destroyed, yet in my flesh I will see God; I myself will see him with my own eyes—I, and not another. How my heart yearns within me!"

Job 19:25–27

For Discussion

1. Did God ever tell Job why he afflicted him? Discuss the implications of this.
2. How did seeing God face-to-face change Job?
3. What postures and attitudes are appropriate when you are in the presence of God?
4. Job probably lived long before Moses and would not have had any of the Bible to read. Discuss how your attitude and words ought to be different from Job's because you have God's revelation of himself before you in the book of Job and in the rest of the Bible.

"All Praise to God, Who Reigns Above"

Then come before his presence now and banish fear and sadness;
To your Redeemer pay your vows and sing with joy and gladness:
Though great distress my soul befell, the Lord, my God, did all things well.
To God all praise and glory.

Johann J. Schütz, 1675

For Further Study

Job 38–42; Isaiah 5:19; Deuteronomy 29:29

21

EMMANUEL'S LAND

Revelation 22

Glory and Oxygen

Nearly fifty years ago, my grandfather stood anxiously beside the deathbed of my great-grandfather in the small coastal hospital in Hoquiam, Washington. Like most men of his generation, Charles Wesley Bond could do and had done anything that needed doing. Though surrounded by hardworking and hard-living loggers and millworkers, my great-grandfather had lived a careful Christian life. For his zealous sharing of the gospel, he was called "the Preacher" by his neighbors.

Though he had been unresponsive for several days, and the doctors gave the family no hope of recovery, he suddenly opened his eyes and raised his hands toward heaven. As my father told the story, a look of recognition and wonder spread across his features, and he said, "Glory! Glory!" and died.

My great-grandfather's death reminds me of Stephen, who "looked up to heaven and saw the glory of God, and Jesus standing at the right hand of God. 'Look,' he said, 'I see heaven open and the Son of Man standing at the right hand of God' " (Acts 7:55–56). My great-grandfather's final word also makes me profoundly grateful for God's faithfulness to his promise to be the God of his children's children.

I'm equally grateful for my last conversation with my grandfather, Elmer Elwood Bond, when he was ninety-one years old. He was lonely for my grandmother, who had died some years before, and weary of the world. "Dougie," he said, hands clasped behind his back, as we slowly walked along the corridor of his assisted-living facility, "I'm homesick for heaven."

After two and a half years of chemotherapy, a stem-cell transplant, radiation, and sixteen bone-marrow biopsies, my father was in what doctors call "final-stage leukemia." He had a series of mini-strokes in the days before he died. After one of them as he slowly regained consciousness, he looked bewildered, and asked what time it was. I told him it was getting closer to time for heaven, and that in heaven he wouldn't go up to Paul or Moses, or Bunyan or Spurgeon, or Jesus, and ask what time it was. I felt his hand faintly squeeze mine, and he smiled.

Then a strange thing happened. His bewilderment disappeared; he seemed to relax, and a look of profound peace came over him. As he struggled to speak, what came from his lips were words of gratitude and praise. "So blessed," he repeated several times.

A day or two later, his final word was "oxygen," and then he died. I'll admit, at first I felt let down that his final word was just "oxygen," and I ached that he had had to suffer so much. Then, as a balm to my grief in the days after he died, it occurred to me how similar my Lord's dying words were: "I thirst."

Heaven Means Dying

Talk of heaven used to make me pretty uncomfortable. Read a passage such as the last chapter of the Bible and it all sounds overwhelmingly wonderful, beyond imagining, thrilling beyond words.

Still, for most young men, the nagging uneasiness persists. Sit by your father's bedside as he calls for oxygen and then dies, and there's good reason for the uneasiness.

I remember avoiding deep conversation with my parents about heaven and longings to go there that from time to time flickered on my affections; I was afraid that if I told them my warmest thoughts about heaven, those words would become self-fulfilling premonitions, and they would be retelling them at my funeral a few days later.

And there's the clincher. It wasn't heaven itself that I had the aversion to; it was what I had to pass through to get there that made me uneasy. Columnist George F. Will tells the story of a cleric who, when "asked how one might come to understand the Church's teaching on Heaven and Hell, answered succinctly: 'Die.'" There's the rub. It was dying that made me try to suppress thoughts of heaven, and dying makes a young man rather uneasy. Check that. It makes most young men nothing short of terrified. Thus, as a teenager, I pushed thoughts of dying—and of heaven—as far into the future as I could, so far that for long stretches I deluded myself into thinking it would never happen at all.

I did this, and you do this, for a reason. Today, young men are usually healthy, full of life, strong, ambitious. You may even feel invincible and imagine that you contain the world, that you will always be "in the pink," as Edwardian English gentlemen glibly termed it.

But if you lived in any other century than you do, or in any other part of the world than you do, you would not be so inclined to think this way. One hundred years ago the average man lived to be only forty-eight years old, and one out of ten babies died before they were a year old. Go further back in history, and mortality rates soared higher still. Saintly Samuel Rutherford lost six children and his wife before his own death in 1661.

Or review the rare Huguenot church records from Rouen after a wave of *le contagion* swept through the congregation. Imagine the grief and anguish of Louise Simon when her husband Guillaume died and was buried on October 22, 1635. Three days later, still reeling from her loss, she must bury her daughter Marion, and three days after that she must bury her ten-year-old daughter Jeanne and on the same day her eighteen-year-old, Elizabeth. The rough wind still blew. Not four days later she would bury yet another daughter, Marguerite.

Life was filled with pain and loss in those days, and so it is for many Christians today who suffer disease and persecution. But admit it. All this is galaxies away from your life and experience. Read the history; watch the news reports of suffering around the globe—none of it really sinks in.

Heaven on Earth

Most young men are full of energy, curiosity, and enthusiasm. You have friends and sports, and most of you have prosperity and lots of toys that contribute to the delusion. You might even be tempted to ask, "How much better can heaven be than all this?" The pleasures of life lie all about you. The familiar things are so full of delight that it's, frankly, difficult to imagine misery, pain, and loss, the constant reminders of reality in virtually all other worlds except yours. And when you've got it all, it's a simple matter to delude yourself into thinking that the good life will last forever.

In the most famous American Puritan sermon, "Sinners in the Hands of an Angry God," preached on July 8, 1741, at second meeting house in Enfield, Connecticut, Jonathan Edwards said that "the children of men miserably delude themselves in confidence in their own strength and wisdom; they trust to nothing but shadow."

Thanks to good things such as modern medicine and free-market economics, the delusion is potent. Unlike in Edwards's time, today young men rarely if ever see sick and dying people. We are surrounded by so much prosperity and pleasure that it's finally difficult to convince ourselves that heaven could be any better.

Life has many foretastes of heaven—even for many unbelievers. But for the Christian, life lived in obedience to God in this world yields rich foretastes of eternal joy in heaven. Puritan preacher and Westminster divine Joseph Caryl observed in 1653 that "all saints shall enjoy a heaven when they leave this earth; some saints enjoy a heaven while they are here on earth." But the danger comes when we grow content with the mere foretastes and begin thinking that joy now is everything. Worse yet, we begin to imagine that money and temporal pleasures are what bring the foretastes. Think that way and it takes only a nudge before you care nothing for heaven. You've come full circle and are back to seeking heaven in earthly things. It's a fruitless search.

One of the problems with earthly pleasures is that they are fleeting. "It was heavenly while it lasted," we say of a walk on the beach at sunset, or a sail in the moonlight, or a plate of Panang curry, or a bowl of favorite ice cream. You name it. The highest pleasure you can find in this life does not last. It's over in a flash.

But not so with heavenly pleasures. "You will fill me with joy in your presence," wrote David in Psalm 16:11, "with eternal pleasures at your right hand." Eternal pleasures—that means that they will last and never fade in intensity, that they will never cease to give you the excitement and thrill, the peaceful relaxation, or the accelerating flood of experience that literally takes your breath away.

See through the Shadows

Nevertheless, it is in our nature to pitch our hopes on what we can see, on the familiar things that gratify us now, and in so doing to pitch our hopes on earth. So how do we make our way through the shadows?

Puritan preacher Richard Baxter faced the same question in his parish in Kidderminster and wrote of it in his most enduring book, *Saints' Everlasting Rest*:

> Come to a man who hath the world at will and tell him, "This is not your happiness; you have higher things to look after," and how little will he regard you! But when affliction comes, it speaks convincingly, and will be heard when preachers cannot. What warm, affectionate, eager thoughts we have of the world till affliction cool them and moderate them! How few and

cold would our thoughts of heaven be, how little should we care for coming thither, if God would give us rest on earth! When the world is worth nothing, then heaven is worth something.

To see clearly here, you and I need to reconnect ourselves with the realities of sickness and death. We need our comfortable thoughts of the world and its pleasures cooled by facing the reality of sin-induced affliction in our fallen world. Then and only then will we be disposed to see and value heaven in proportion to the world's deserts.

While writing this chapter, I was called out in the night to go to the bedside of an eighty-six-year-old member of our congregation, Frank Starr, a World War II combat veteran who fought with the 82nd Airborne. His dear wife called to say that he was not doing well, that he was in intensive care at the veterans hospital in Seattle, Washington, and that the hospital had sent a cab for her. She asked if I would come. The doctor did not sound hopeful. "The CAT scan shows that his lungs are full of clots," he said. "At any moment one of those could dislodge. He is a very sick man."

Surprised that he was breathing so easily, I leaned over him. "How are you, Frank?" I asked. With a twinkle in his eyes, he replied as he had for many years, "Pretty good for a no-good." And then I said, as I had replied to him many times, that I knew someone who made it his business to make no-goods good. "Thank you, Jesus," he replied softly.

The doctor, accustomed to being around dying people, kept commenting on how peaceful Frank was—when the CAT scan looked so grim. Impressive as it is, medical technology is really quite limited. Such things as peace with God, heaven just across the river, eternal pleasures at God's right hand forevermore—none of that registers well on a CAT scan.

Seeing this dear old man hoping in Christ and longing for heaven as he lay afflicted and dying helped me to value heaven more and earth less. The same will be true for you. "Illness sanctified is better than health," observed poet William Cowper. Like Baxter, Cowper understood that affliction, rightly understood, will turn the Christian from deluded contentment with the partial things of this life to wonder and longing for the fullness of heaven—the death of death, eternal joys, pleasures forevermore.

Taking Aim

Many things in a fallen world are counterintuitive. The young man who will have real joy and satisfaction in this life never gets it by striving after earthly things. He must set his face toward the Celestial City, toward heaven. "Aim at Heaven and you get earth thrown in," wrote C. S. Lewis. "Aim at earth and you get neither."

A wise young man—in spite of vigorous health, strength, and a lifetime of opportunity and privilege before him—sets his affections on things above and lays up treasures in heaven, treasures that can never be taken away, that never fade or rust or betray, and that satisfy now and forever. Set your sights on earthly pleasures and you'll consume your life in the futile pursuit of rainbows—but never find a single one.

A thoughtful young man must begin early to establish a clear sight of heaven. This demands that you unmask the familiar things that cloud your vision. You must grow up in faith and be a man in order to set your sights on heaven, and then you must order your life with a view to getting there, whatever the cost.

The fundamental problem for most young men is that they set their sights only on what they can see right now. They imagine that health and prosperity will last forever, that their lungs will never be full of blood clots, that only other people get cancer, that only old people die, that life now is as good as heaven. Brace yourself like a man. Unmask the delusion. Expose the fraud. It's all a lie. Stop believing it!

Speak to yourself like John Bunyan's Mr. Standfast as he faced dying and the Celestial City just beyond:

> The thoughts of what I am going to, and of the conduct that waits for me on the other side, doth lie as a glowing coal at my heart. I see myself now at the end of my journey; my toilsome days are ended. I am going now to see that head that was crowned with thorns, and that face which was spit upon for me. I have formerly lived by hearsay and faith: but now I go where I shall live by sight, and shall be with Him in whose company I delight myself.

Do you delight yourself in the company of Jesus? Do you practice the spiritual disciplines that put you in the company of Jesus: daily prayer, Bible reading and meditation, heartfelt and manly singing of praise to God, fellowship and godly conversation? Heaven will be eternal pleasure because you will be in the company of King Jesus. Practice the presence of Christ in your daily life, in your entertainments, in your friendships, and you will be fitting yourself for heaven.

Be ruthless with entertainments that focus your sights on the easy-come, easy-go frivolities that pass for pleasure in this life. Cut off the music or movies or friends that support the delusion that you need to live for the immediate gratification found in worldly things. An important way to do this is to take your stand with friends like Mr. Standfast—and hold fast with them to the end. The Bible is full of such men—Joshua, Job, Peter, Paul—and so is church history.

Farewell, World

On December 22, 1666, after a month of prison and torture, young Covenanter preacher Hugh M'Kail, flanked by the king's soldiers, staggered through the gray streets of Edinburgh. M'Kail had been arrested and condemned to death for complicity in the Battle of Rullion Green, a well-intentioned but disastrous stand taken by farmers in defense of "the Crown rights of the Redeemer in his Kirk." Few among them were trained soldiers, and only a handful carried muskets or basket-hilt claymores. It had all begun in Galloway when a handful of farmers attempted to defend an old man against the unjust brutalities of the king's dragoons. M'Kail had joined the Pentland Rising, as the king's Privy Counsel called it, as chaplain and preacher.

Now the pale young minister paused at the foot of the scaffold, and after declaring that he'd seen in his condemnation "a clear ray of the majesty of the Lord," he sang the thirty-first Psalm. His body racked with pain from weeks of torture, he mounted the first step of the scaffold and said, "I care no more to go up this ladder, and over it, than if I were going to my father's house." At the next agonizing step he paused. "Every step is a degree nearer heaven."

When he finally reached the top, he took out his Bible and read from the last chapter. "And he showed me a pure river of life, clear as crystal, proceeding out of the throne of God and of the Lamb . . ." After encouraging the faithful, he prayed: "Now I leave off to speak any more to creatures, and turn my speech to thee, O Lord. Now I begin a conversation with God, which shall never be broken off. Farewell, father and mother, friends and relations! Farewell, the world and all delights! Farewell, meat and drink! Farewell, sun, moon and stars!"

A hush fell over the crowds; even the king's dragoons were silent, and the fervent young man's prayer was not drowned out by drum-rolling. M'Kail continued: "Welcome, God and Father! Welcome, sweet Lord Jesus, Mediator of the New Covenant! Welcome, blessed Spirit of grace, God of all consolation! Welcome, glory! Welcome, eternal life—!"

His prayer was cut off as the hangman tightened the noose around his neck. Hugh M'Kail's confidence at the gallows reminds me of renowned Bible commentator Matthew Henry's statement, "He whose head is in heaven need not fear to put his feet into the grave."

All this is what the Puritans called dying grace, but you don't get it by setting your sights on earth. You prepare to die well, like a man, by "setting your affections on things above" (see Col. 3:2), by cultivating a love and longing for heaven. Only then are you prepared to live your life to the hilt and to die hoping confidently in Christ, as M'Kail did.

Live life aiming at glory, as my great-grandfather did, and you will get bits of heaven now—and eternal pleasures forever after. "For we have become partakers of Christ, if we hold fast the beginning of our assurance firm until the end" (Heb. 3:14 NASB).

Prayer Resolves

- To cultivate a clearer sight of heaven by reading and meditating on biblical passages about dying and heaven
- To cut off entertainments and influences that conflict with seeing and longing for heaven
- To lay up treasure in heaven by loving God and loving and serving my neighbor for his sake

Scripture Memory

"I am unworthy—how can I reply to you? I put my hand over my mouth."

Job 40:4

For Discussion

1. Discuss the times when you have experienced the clearest sight of heaven.
2. Discuss the times when heaven seems remote.
3. What were you doing or reading or watching or thinking about in each case?
4. Now discuss a strategy to keep the reality of heaven before your mind and heart.

"The Sands of Time Are Sinking"

The King there in his beauty
Without a veil is seen;
It were a well-spent journey
Though sev'n deaths lay between:
The Lamb with his fair army
Doth on Mount Zion stand,
And glory, glory dwelleth
In Emmanuel's land.

Anne R. Cousin (from letters of Samuel Rutherford), 1857

For Further Study

1 Thessalonians 4:13–18; meditate on the hymn "There Is a Land of Pure Delight," by Isaac Watts; read the final letter of *The Screwtape Letters*, by C. S. Lewis

SELECT BIBLIOGRAPHY FOR FURTHER READING

Confessions, St. Augustine
Saints' Everlasting Rest, Richard Baxter
The Letters of Robert Murray M'Cheyne, Andrew Bonar
Grace Abounding to the Chief of Sinners, John Bunyan
The Pilgrim's Progress, John Bunyan
Commentary on Paul's Epistle to the Romans, John Calvin
Institutes of the Christian Religion, John Calvin
Letters of John Calvin, John Calvin
Personal Narrative, Jonathan Edwards
To a Rising Generation, Jonathan Edwards
C. T. Studd: Athlete and Pioneer, Norman P. Grubb
Scots Worthies, John Howie
Letters to Malcolm, C. S. Lewis
Mere Christianity, C. S. Lewis
Surprised by Joy, C. S. Lewis
The Abolition of Man, C. S. Lewis
The Chronicles of Narnia, C. S. Lewis
The Screwtape Letters, C. S. Lewis
Till We Have Faces, C. S. Lewis
The Plight of Man and the Power of God, D. Martyn Lloyd-Jones

SELECT BIBLIOGRAPHY

The Bondage of the Will, Martin Luther
Mortification of Sin, John Owen
Evangelism and the Sovereignty of God, J. I. Packer
Knowing God, J. I. Packer
Pensées, Blaise Pascal
Amusing Ourselves to Death, Neil Postman
Letters, Samuel Rutherford
Trial and Triumph of Faith, Samuel Rutherford
Worldly Saints, Leland Ryken
City on a Hill, Philip Graham Ryken
Give Praise to God, Philip Graham Ryken, Derek W. H. Thomas, and
    J. Ligon Duncan
My Father's World, Philip Graham Ryken
Practical Religion, J. C. Ryle
Thoughts for Young Men, J. C. Ryle
The Complete Works, William Shakespeare
Morning and Evening, Charles Haddon Spurgeon
Sermons, Charles Haddon Spurgeon
Statesman and Saint: The Principled Politics of William Wilberforce,
    David J. Vaughan
Logic, Isaac Watts
Lord, Teach Us to Pray, Alexander Whyte

A YOUNG MAN'S HYMNAL, VOLUME 2

Men are less interested in attending church regularly and even less inclined to commit themselves to ministry responsibilities and leadership in the church in part because there is a significant shift in how Christians worship. Relational songs and emotive choruses have replaced the strong, manly hymns that were sung by men and boys and their families in worship for millenniums. Instead of stout hymns about battles, and triumphant psalms about conquering enemies, and doctrinal poetry calling men to base their lives and deeds on solid biblical foundations, the contemporary church sings superficial songs that make real men feel like they have to act like women in order to be Christians. Young men who grow up under pressure to sing breathy, feminine songs in worship will never be spiritually, intellectually, and emotionally capable of godly leadership in their homes, in Christ's church, or in the world. The following collection of hymns will help men "be done with lesser things" and lift their voices in Christ-honoring, manly worship. (Visit www.cyberhymnal.org and www.pjonesmusic.us for tunes to many of these hymns.)

- All People That on Earth Do Dwell (W. Kethe)
- And Can It Be? (C. Wesley)

- Be Thou My Vision (D. Forgaill)
- Come, Bless the Lord and Trembling Rise (D. Bond)
- Creator God, Our Sovereign Lord (D. Bond)
- Father, I Know That All My Life (A. Waring)
- Fear Not, O Little Flock, the Foe (J. Altenburg)
- Glorious Things of Thee Are Spoken (J. Newton)
- How Sweet and Awful Is the Place (I. Watts)
- I Love Thy Kingdom, Lord (T. Dwight)
- If I Can Speak in Tongues of Fire (D. Bond)
- It Is Well with My Soul (H. Spafford)
- Jesus, Priceless Treasure (J. Franck)
- King Jesus Reigns (D. Bond)
- Lift High the Cross (G. Kitchin)
- My Song Is Love Unknown (S. Crossman)
- None Other Lamb (C. Rossetti)
- O God, My Faithful God (J. Heermann)
- O Love of God, How Strong and True (H. Bonar)
- O Sacred Head, Now Wounded (B. of Clairvaux)
- O the Deep, Deep Love of Jesus (S. T. Francis)
- Of the Father's Love Begotten (A. Prudentius)
- Our God in All Things Works for Good (D. Bond)
- Our God, Our Help in Ages Past (I. Watts)
- Praise, My Soul, the King of Heaven (H. Lyte)
- Rock of Ages, Cleft for Me (A. Toplady)
- See, the Conqueror Mounts in Triumph (C. Wordsworth)
- Stand Up and Bless the Lord (J. Montgomery)
- The Lord's My Shepherd, I'll Not Want (Psalm 23, Scottish Psalter)
- The Sands of Time Are Sinking (A. Cousin/S. Rutherford)
- This Day at Thy Creating Word (W. How)
- Triumphant Jesus Bore the Cross (D. Bond)
- We Rise and Worship (D. Bond)
- What Wondrous Love Is This? (A. Means)
- When I Survey the Wondrous Cross (I. Watts)

All people that on earth do dwell,
Sing to the Lord with cheerful voice.
Him serve with fear, his praise forth tell;
Come ye before him and rejoice.

The Lord, ye know, is God indeed;
Without our aid he did us make;
We are his folk, he doth us feed,
And for his sheep he doth us take.

O enter then his gates with praise;
Approach with joy his courts unto;
Praise, laud, and bless his name always,
For it is seemly so to do.

For why? the Lord our God is good;
His mercy is for ever sure;
His truth at all times firmly stood,
And shall from age to age endure.

Words: William Kethe, 1561
Tune: OLD HUNDREDTH, Louis Bourgeois, 1551

And can it be that I should gain
An int'rest in the Savior's blood?
Died he for me, who caused his pain?
For me, who him to death pursued?
Amazing love! How can it be
That thou, my God, shouldst die for me?

'Tis myst'ry all! Th'Immortal dies:
Who can explore his strange design?
In vain the firstborn seraph tries

To sound the depths of love divine.
'Tis mercy all! Let earth adore,
Let angel minds inquire no more.

He left his Father's throne above
(So free, so infinite his grace!),
Humbled himself (so great his love!),
And bled for all his chosen race.
'Tis mercy all, immense and free;
For, O my God, it found out me.

Long my imprisoned spirit lay
Fast bound in sin and nature's night;
Thine eye diffused a quick'ning ray;
I woke, the dungeon flamed with light;
My chains fell off, my heart was free;
I rose, went forth, and followed thee.

No condemnation now I dread;
Jesus, and all in him, is mine!
Alive in him, my living Head,
And clothed in righteousness divine,
Bold I approach th'eternal throne,
And claim the crown, through Christ, my own.

Words: Charles Wesley, 1738
Tune: SAGINA, Thomas Campbell, 1825

Be thou my Vision, O Lord of my heart;
Naught be all else to me, save that thou art.
Thou my best Thought, by day or by night,
Waking or sleeping, thy presence my light.

Be thou my Wisdom, and thou my true Word;
I ever with thee and thou with me, Lord;
Thou my great Father, I thy true son;
Thou in me dwelling, and I with thee one.

Be thou my battle Shield, Sword for the fight;
Be thou my Dignity, thou my Delight;
Thou my soul's Shelter, thou my high Tower:
Raise thou me heavenward, O Power of my power.

Riches I heed not, nor man's empty praise,
Thou mine Inheritance, now and always:
Thou and thou only, first in my heart,
High King of Heaven, my Treasure thou art.

High King of Heaven, my victory won,
May I reach Heaven's joys, O bright Heaven's Sun!
Heart of my own heart, whatever befall,
Still be my Vision, O Ruler of all.

Words: Dallan Forgaill, 8th century
Tune: SLANE, Irish folk tune, 433

◆ ◆ ◆

Come, bless the Lord and trembling rise
Before the Sovereign of the skies;
Before his majesty now raise
Adoring hymns of grateful praise!

Bow humbly down, your sins confess;
Pour out your soul, on mercy rest.
Since Christ triumphant bears your woe,
Repent, his cleansing mercy know.

Rise joyful now and Jesus bless
For his imputed righteousness,
His sovereign kindness, lavished grace,
His freely dying in your place.

Pay all your vows and cheerful bring
The gifts he gave; give back to him.
His gifts, so vast, his life outpoured—
Ourselves we lay before you, Lord.

Come, Word of Life, yourself reveal;
Your truth make us to know and feel;
Inflame our minds to love your ways;
Make us a sacrifice of praise.

Come, Jesus Christ, sweet heav'nly Bread,
And with your life this table spread,
Then grateful we will solemn dine
On hallowed bread and sacred wine.

Now go into the world in peace,
And bear the burdens of the least,
And bathe your neighbors' feet in love,
So Christ they'll know and praise above.

Words: Douglas Bond, June 4, 2008
Tune: SHIRLEY STREET, Ronald Jay Bechtel, 2008

Creator God, our Sovereign Lord,
The heavens tell, the stars have shown,
Your splendor, might, and Deity,
But Truth lies in your Word alone.
        My heart to you, O God, I give,
        And by your Word I live.

In Truth your Word reveals my guilt,
My lost, unworthy self makes known,
But now made new I'm justified
And live and move by Faith alone.
      My heart to you, O God, I give,
      And now by Faith I live.

Before you made the world you chose,
In love, to send your only Son
To ransom me and make me one
With Christ, my Lord, by Grace alone.
      My heart to you, O God, I give,
      And now by Grace I live.

O Christ, Redeemer, Savior, King,
Subdued by grace, I am your own;
Enthrall my soul and make me free,
Reformed, redeemed by Christ alone.
      My heart to you, O God, I give,
      And now in Christ I live.

O glorious God, who reigns on high,
With heart in hand, before your throne,
We hymn your glory 'round the world
With psalms adoring you alone.
      My heart to you, O God, I give
      And for your glory live.

Words: Douglas Bond, 2007
Tune: Cor Meum Tibi Offero, Paul S. Jones, 2008

Father, I know that all my life
Is portioned out for me;

The changes that are sure to come
I do not fear to see;

I ask thee for a present mind
Intent on pleasing thee.

I would not have the restless will
That hurries to and fro,
Seeking for some great thing to do
Or secret thing to know;
I would be treated as a child,
And guided where I go.

I ask thee for the daily strength,
To none that ask denied,
A mind to blend with outward life
While keeping at thy side;
Content to fill a little space,
If thou be glorified.

In service which thy will appoints
There are no bonds for me;
My inmost heart is taught the truth
That makes thy children free.
A life of self-renouncing love
Is one of liberty.

Words: Anna Waring, 1850
Tune: Morwellham, Charles Steggall, 1826–1905

Fear not, O little flock, the foe
Who madly seeks your overthrow;
Dread not his rage and power:

What though your courage sometimes faints,
His seeming triumph o'er God's saints
Lasts but a little hour.
Be of good cheer; your cause belongs
To him who can avenge your wrongs;
Leave it to him, our Lord:
Though hidden yet from all our eyes,
He sees the Gideon who shall rise
To save us and his Word.

As true as God's own Word is true,
Nor earth nor hell with all their crew
Against us shall prevail.
A jest and byword are they grown;
God is with us, we are his own;
Our vict'ry cannot fail.

Amen, Lord Jesus, grant our pray'r;
Great Captain, now your arm make bare,
Fight for us once again;
So shall your saints and martyrs raise
A mighty chorus to your praise,
World without end. Amen.

Words: Johann Michael Altenburg, 1584–1640
Tune: Jehovah Nissi, Edward Patrick Crawford, 1846–1912

Glorious things of thee are spoken,
Zion, city of our God!
He, whose Word cannot be broken,
Formed thee for his own abode.
On the Rock of Ages founded,
What can shake thy sure repose?

With salvation's walls surrounded,
Thou may'st smile at all thy foes.

See! the streams of living waters,
Springing from eternal love;
Well supply thy sons and daughters,
And all fear of want remove:
Who can faint while such a river
Ever flows their thirst t'assuage?
Grace, which like the Lord, the Giver,
Never fails from age to age.

'Round each habitation hovering,
See the cloud and fire appear!
For a glory and a cov'ring
Showing that the Lord is near.
Thus deriving from our banner
Light by night and shade by day;
Safe they feed upon the manna
Which he gives them when they pray.

Savior, if of Zion's city,
I through grace a member am,
Let the world deride or pity,
I will glory in thy Name.
Fading is the worldling's pleasure,
All his boasted pomp and show;
Solid joys and lasting treasure
None but Zion's children know.

Words: John Newton, 1779
Tune: AUSTRIA, Franz Joseph Haydn, 1797

How sweet and awful is the place
With Christ within the doors,

While everlasting love displays
The choicest of her stores!

While all our hearts and all our songs
Join to admire the feast,
Each of us cries, with thankful tongues,
"Lord, why was I a guest?

"Why was I made to hear thy voice,
And enter while there's room,
When thousands make a wretched choice,
And rather starve than come?"

'Twas the same love that spread the feast
That sweetly drew us in;
Else we had still refused to taste,
And perished in our sin.

Pity the nations, O our God!
Constrain the earth to come;
Send thy victorious Word abroad,
And bring the strangers home.

We long to see thy churches full,
That all the chosen race
May with one voice, and heart and soul,
Sing thy redeeming grace.

Words: Isaac Watts, 1707
Tune: ST. COLUMBA, Ancient Irish melody

◆ ◆ ◆

I love thy kingdom, Lord,
The house of thine abode,
The church our blest Redeemer saved
With his own precious blood.

I love thy church, O God.
Her walls before thee stand,
Dear as the apple of thine eye,
And written on thy hand.

For her my tears shall fall,
For her my prayers ascend,
To her my cares and toils be giv'n
Till toils and cares shall end.

Beyond my highest joy
I prize her heav'nly ways,
Her sweet communion, solemn vows,
Her hymns of love and praise.

Jesus, thou Friend divine,
Our Savior and our King,
Thy hand from every snare and foe
Shall great deliverance bring.

Sure as thy truth shall last,
To Zion shall be giv'n
The brightest glories earth can yield
And brighter bliss of heav'n.

Words: Timothy Dwight, 1800
Tune: ST. THOMAS (WILLIAMS), Aaron Williams, 1770

If I can speak in tongues of fire
Yet fail to do what love requires
I'm nothing—though high mountains move—
I'm nothing without perfect love.

I'm nothing if I try to hide
Resentment, envy, selfish pride.
I'm nothing—though high myst'ries find—
If I'm not patient, humble, kind.

His heav'nly gifts God gives to me
So Christ's perfected love I'd see
And know—and speak, and serve and give—
And like my holy Bridegroom live.

In faith and hope, love perseveres,
No anger and no rudeness hears;
Such loving-kindness—fully blest—
Gives foretastes of eternal rest.

I see in part like children here,
A poor reflection in a mirror;
Yet in my heart I long to find
Love more by Jesus' love refined.

Above I'll know, as Christ has known,
How vast his love for sinners shown!
With eyes undimmed I'll end my race
And gaze on Jesus face-to-face!

Words: Douglas Bond, 2007
Tune: Rothesay, Paul S. Jones, 2008

When peace, like a river, attendeth my way,
When sorrows like sea billows roll;
Whatever my lot, thou hast taught me to say,
It is well, it is well with my soul.

Refrain:
It is well with my soul,
It is well with my soul,
It is well, it is well with my soul.

Though Satan should buffet, though trials should come,
Let this blest assurance control,
That Christ has regarded my helpless estate,
And hath shed his own blood for my soul.
Refrain

My sin, oh, the bliss of this glorious thought!
My sin, not in part but the whole,
Is nailed to the cross, and I bear it no more,
Praise the Lord, praise the Lord, O my soul!
Refrain

And Lord, haste the day when my faith shall be sight,
The clouds be rolled back as a scroll;
The trump shall resound, and the Lord shall descend,
Even so, it is well with my soul.
Refrain

Words: Horatio G. Spafford, 1873
Tune: VILLE DU HAVRE, Philip P. Bliss, 1876

Jesus, priceless Treasure,
Source of purest pleasure,
Truest Friend to me.
Ah, how long in anguish
Shall my spirit languish,
Yearning, Lord, for thee?
Thou art mine, O Lamb divine!
I will suffer naught to hide thee,
Naught I ask beside thee.

In thine arms I rest me;
Foes who would molest me
Cannot reach me here.
Though the earth be shaking,
Every heart be quaking,
Jesus calms my fear.
Lightnings flash and thunders crash;
Yet, though sin and hell assail me,
Jesus will not fail me.

Satan, I defy thee;
Death, I now decry thee;
Fear, I bid thee cease.
World, thou shalt not harm me
Nor thy threats alarm me
While I sing of peace.
God's great power guards every hour;
Earth and all its depths adore him,
Silent bow before him.

Evil world, I leave thee;
Thou canst not deceive me,
Thine appeal is vain.

Sin that once did bind me,
Get thee far behind me,
Come not forth again.
Past thy hour, O pride and power;
Sinful life, thy bonds I sever,
Leave thee now forever.
Hence, with fear and sadness!
For the Lord of gladness,
Jesus, enters in.
Those who love the Father,
Though the storms may gather,
Still have peace within;
Yea, whate'er we here must bear,
Still in thee lies purest pleasure,
Jesus, priceless Treasure!

Words: Johann Franck, 1655
Tune: JESU, MEINE FREUDE, Johann Crüger, 1649

King Jesus reigns, enthroned on high!
We lift our voice and glorify
His Majesty, his power and grace,
And his high sovereignty embrace.

Though kings usurp and proud men try
Their pompous selves to deify,
Adoring praise shall never cease
For Christ, Redeemer, Prince of Peace!

King Jesus rules upon his throne
And does the wealth of nations own;
While fading things to Caesar bring,
Ourselves we render to our King.

While pharaohs, kings, and emperors boast,
The King of kings leads out his host;
The proud, one day, shall bow the knee
When Christ in triumph sets us free!

King Jesus wears his worthy crown,
Though envious men and nations frown,
And we, by grace, on eagle's wings,
Uphold the Crown rights of our King!

His holy nation, chosen ones,
We joyful bow, and with our tongues
We hymn allegiance high and sing,
"Hail Jesus! Sovereign Lord and King!"

Words: Douglas Bond, 2008
Tune: JASPER, Paul S. Jones, 2008

Refrain:
Lift high the cross,
The love of Christ proclaim,
Till all the world adore
His sacred name.

Come, brethren, follow where our Savior trod,
Our King victorious, Christ, the Son of God.

Refrain

Led on their way by this triumphant sign,
The hosts of God in conqu'ring ranks combined.

Refrain

O Lord, once lifted on the glorious tree,
As thou hast promised, draw men unto thee.

Refrain

Thy kingdom come, that earth's despair may cease
Beneath the shadow of its healing peace.

Refrain

For thy blest cross which doth for us atone,
Creation's praises rise before thy throne.

Refrain

Words: George W. Kitchin, 1887
Tune: Crucifer, Sydney H. Nicholson, 1916

My song is love unknown,
My Savior's love to me;
Love to the loveless shown,
That they might lovely be.
O who am I, that for my sake
My Lord should take frail flesh and die?

He came from his blest throne
Salvation to bestow;
But men made strange, and none
The longed-for Christ would know:
But O! my Friend, my Friend indeed,

Who at my need his life did spend.
Sometimes they strew his way,
And his sweet praises sing;
Resounding all the day
Hosannas to their King:
Then "Crucify!" is all their breath,
And for his death they thirst and cry.

Why, what hath my Lord done?
What makes this rage and spite?
He made the lame to run,
He gave the blind their sight.
Sweet injuries! Yet they at these
Themselves displease, and 'gainst him rise.

They rise and needs will have
My dear Lord made away;
A murderer they saved,
The Prince of life they slay,
Yet cheerful he to suffering goes,
That he his foes from thence might free.

In life, no house, no home
My Lord on earth might have;
In death no friendly tomb
But what a stranger gave.
What may I say? Heav'n was his home;
But mine the tomb wherein he lay.

Here might I stay and sing,
No story so divine;
Never was love, dear King!
Never was grief like thine.

This is my Friend, in whose sweet praise
I all my days could gladly spend.

Words: Samuel Crossman, 1664
Tune: St. John (Parish), William Havergal, 1851

None other Lamb, none other Name,
None other hope in heav'n or earth or sea,
None other hiding place from guilt and shame,
None beside Thee!

My faith burns low, my hope burns low;
Only my heart's desire cries out in me
By the deep thunder of its want and woe,
Cries out to thee.

Lord, thou art Life, though I be dead;
Love's fire thou art, however cold I be:
Nor heav'n have I, nor place to lay my head,
Nor home, but thee.

Words: Christina Rossetti, 1907
Tune: All Hallows (Wiseman), Frederick Wiseman, 1858

O God, my faithful God,
True fountain ever flowing,
Without whom nothing is,
All perfect gifts bestowing:
Give me a healthy frame,
And may I have within

A conscience free from blame,
A soul unstained by sin.

Give me the strength to do
With ready heart and willing,
Whatever you command,
My calling here fulfilling—
To do it when I ought,
With all my strength and bless
Whatever I have wrought,
For you must grant success.

Keep me from saying words
That later need recalling;
Guard me lest idle speech
May from my lips be falling:
But when, within my place,
I must and ought to speak,
Then to my words give grace,
Lest I offend the weak.

When dangers gather 'round,
Oh, keep me calm and fearless;
Help me to bear the cross
When life seems dark and cheerless;
Help me, as you have taught,
To love both great and small,
And, by your Spirit's might,
To live at peace with all.

Words: Johann Heermann, 1585–1647
Tune: DARMSTADT, Ahasuerus Fritsch, 1679, arranged by Johann
Sebastian Bach, 1685–1750, in *Cantata 45*

◆ ◆ ◆

O love of God, how strong and true!
Eternal, and yet ever new;
Uncomprehended and unbought,
Beyond all knowledge and all thought.

O love of God, how deep and great!
Far deeper than man's deepest hate;
Self-fed, self-kindled, like the light,
Changeless, eternal, infinite.

O heavenly love, how precious still,
In days of weariness and ill,
In nights of pain and helplessness,
To heal, to comfort, and to bless!

O wide-embracing, wondrous love!
We read thee in the sky above,
We read thee in the earth below,
In seas that swell, and streams that flow.

We read thee best in him who came
To bear for us the cross of shame;
Sent by the Father from on high,
Our life to live, our death to die.

We read thy power to bless and save,
E'en in the darkness of the grave;
Still more in resurrection light,
We read the fullness of thy might.

O love of God, our shield and stay
Through all the perils of our way!

Eternal love, in thee we rest
Forever safe, forever blest.

Words: Horatius Bonar, 1858
Tune: JERUSALEM (PARRY), C. Hubert H. Parry, 1916, arranged by
Janet Wyatt, 1977

O sacred Head, now wounded,
With grief and shame weighed down;
Now scornfully surrounded with thorns,
Thine only crown;
O sacred Head, what glory,
What bliss till now was thine!
Yet, though despised and gory,
I joy to call thee mine.

What thou, my Lord, hast suffered
Was all for sinners' gain:
Mine, mine was the transgression,
But thine the deadly pain.
Lo, here I fall, my Savior!
'Tis I deserve thy place;
Look on me with thy favor,
Vouchsafe to me thy grace.

What language shall I borrow
To thank thee, dearest Friend,
For this, thy dying sorrow,
Thy pity without end?
O make me thine forever;
And should I fainting be,

Lord, let me never, never
Outlive my love to thee.

Words: Bernard of Clairvaux, 1091–1153
Tune: PASSION CHORALE, Hans Leo Hassler, 1601

O the deep, deep love of Jesus, vast, unmeasured, boundless, free!
Rolling as a mighty ocean in its fullness over me!
Underneath me, all around me, is the current of thy love
Leading onward, leading homeward to thy glorious rest above!

O the deep, deep love of Jesus, spread his praise from shore to shore!
How he loveth, ever loveth, changeth never, nevermore!
How he watches o'er his loved ones, died to call them all his own;
How for them he intercedeth, watcheth o'er them from the throne!

O the deep, deep love of Jesus, love of every love the best!
'Tis an ocean full of blessing, 'tis a haven giving rest!
O the deep, deep love of Jesus, 'tis a heav'n of heav'ns to me;
And it lifts me up to glory, for it lifts me up to thee!

Words: Samuel Trevor Francis, 1875
Tune: EBENEZER, Thomas J. Williams, 1890

Of the Father's love begotten, ere the worlds began to be,
He is Alpha and Omega, he the source, the ending he,
Of the things that are, that have been,
And that future years shall see, evermore and evermore!

O that birth forever blessèd, when the virgin, full of grace,
By the Holy Ghost conceiving, bare the Savior of our race;

And the Babe, the world's Redeemer,
First revealed his sacred face, evermore and evermore!

This is he whom seers in old time chanted of with one accord;
Whom the voices of the prophets promised in their faithful word;
Now he shines, the long-expected,
Let creation praise its Lord, evermore and evermore!

O ye heights of heaven adore him; angel hosts, his praises sing;
Powers, dominions, bow before him, and extol our God and King!
Let no tongue on earth be silent,
Every voice in concert ring, evermore and evermore!

Christ, to thee with God the Father, and, O Holy Ghost, to thee,
Hymn and chant with high thanksgiving, and unwearied praises be:
Honor, glory, and dominion,
And eternal victory, evermore and evermore!

Words: Aurelius Prudentius, 5th century
Tune: DIVINUM MYSTERIUM, Sanctus Trope, 11th century

Our God in all things works for good;
His sovereign purposes have stood,
And will through endless ages stand,
Sustained and ordered by his hand.

In goodness God stretched out the sky,
The sun and moon and stars that cry,
"Almighty God has made all things!"
Creation groans yet shouts and sings.

From heaven's bounty God gives food
To saint and rebel, bad and good;

This God in all things meets men's needs
And just and unjust kindly feeds.

When clouds descend and troubles rise,
Distress, and darkness, death and cries,
Still God is good in pain and loss,
And bears his own who bear their cross.

Redeeming goodness, from the fall,
For chosen ones he bought and called,
In goodness to repentance leads,
His lambs God draws, and heals, and feeds.

Yes, God in all things works for good;
His loving-kindness firm has stood,
And will through endless ages stand,
Unerring, ordered by his hand.

Words: Douglas Bond, 2006
Tune: BRYNTEG, John A. Lloyd Sr., 1815–74

Our God, our help in ages past,
Our hope for years to come,
Our shelter from the stormy blast,
And our eternal home.

Under the shadow of thy throne
Thy saints have dwelt secure;
Sufficient is thine arm alone,
And our defense is sure.

Before the hills in order stood,
Or earth received her frame,

From everlasting thou art God,
To endless years the same.

A thousand ages in thy sight
Are like an evening gone;
Short as the watch that ends the night
Before the rising sun.

The busy tribes of flesh and blood,
With all their lives and cares,
Are carried downward by the flood,
And lost in following years.

Time, like an ever-rolling stream,
Bears all her sons away;
They fly, forgotten, as a dream
Dies at the opening day.

Our God, our help in ages past,
Our hope for years to come,
Be thou our guard while troubles last,
And our eternal home.

Words: Isaac Watts, 1719
Tune: St. Anne, William Croft, 1708

◆ ◆ ◆

Praise, my soul, the King of heaven;
To his feet thy tribute bring.
Ransomed, healed, restored, forgiven,
Evermore his praises sing:
Alleluia! Alleluia!
Praise the everlasting King.

Praise him for his grace and favor
To our fathers in distress.
Praise him still the same as ever,
Slow to chide, and swift to bless.
Alleluia! Alleluia!
Glorious in his faithfulness.

Fatherlike, he tends and spares us;
Well our feeble frame he knows.
In his hands he gently bears us,
Rescues us from all our foes.
Alleluia! Alleluia!
Widely yet His mercy flows.
Frail as summer's flower we flourish,
Blows the wind and it is gone;
But while mortals rise and perish
Our God lives unchanging on,
Praise him, Praise him, Hallelujah!
Praise the High Eternal One!

Angels, help us to adore him;
Ye behold him face-to-face;
Sun and moon, bow down before him,
Dwellers all in time and space.
Alleluia! Alleluia!
Praise with us the God of grace.

Words: Henry Lyte, 1834
Tune: Lauda Anima, John Goss, 1869

Rock of Ages, cleft for me,
Let me hide myself in thee;
Let the water and the blood,

From thy riven side which flowed,
Be of sin the double cure,
Cleanse me from its guilt and pow'r.

Not the labors of my hands
Can fulfil thy law's demands;
Could my zeal no respite know,
Could my tears forever flow,
All for sin could not atone;
Thou must save, and thou alone.

Nothing in my hand I bring,
Simply to thy cross I cling;
Naked, come to thee for dress;
Helpless, look to thee for grace;
Foul, I to the Fountain fly;
Wash me, Savior, or I die.

While I draw this fleeting breath,
When mine eyelids close in death,
When I soar to worlds unknown,
See thee on thy judgment throne,
Rock of Ages, cleft for me,
Let me hide myself in thee.

Words: Augustus M. Toplady, 1776
Tune: New City Fellowship, James Ward, 1984

See, the Conqueror mounts in triumph; see the King in royal state,
Riding on the clouds, his chariot, to his heavenly palace gate.
Hark! the choirs of angel voices joyful alleluias sing,
And the portals high are lifted to receive their heavenly King.

Who is this that comes in glory, with the trump of jubilee?
Lord of battles, God of armies, he has gained the victory.
He who on the cross did suffer, he who from the grave arose,
He has vanquished sin and Satan, He by death has spoiled His foes.

He has raised our human nature in the clouds to God's right hand;
There we sit in heavenly places, there with him in glory stand:
Jesus reigns, adored by angels; man with God is on the throne;
Mighty Lord, in thine ascension we by faith behold our own.

Raise us up from earth to heaven, give us wings of faith and love,
Gales of holy aspirations wafting us to realms above;

That, with hearts and minds uplifted, we with Christ our Lord may
    dwell,
Where he sits enthroned in glory in his heavenly citadel.

Glory be to God the Father, glory be to God the Son,
Dying, risen, ascending for us, who the heavenly realm has won;
Glory to the Holy Spirit, to one God in persons three;
Glory both in earth and heaven, glory, endless glory, be.

Words: Christopher Wordsworth, 1862
Tune: RUSTINGTON, C. Hubert H. Parry, 1897

Stand up and bless the Lord,
Ye people of his choice;
Stand up and bless the Lord your God
With heart and soul and voice.

Though high above all praise,
Above all blessing high,

Who would not fear his holy Name,
And laud and magnify?

O for the living flame
From his own altar brought,
To touch our lips, our minds inspire,
And wing to heaven our thought!

God is our Strength and Song,
And his salvation ours;
Then be his love in Christ proclaimed
With all our ransomed powers.
Stand up and bless the Lord;
The Lord your God adore;
Stand up and bless his glorious Name;
Henceforth forevermore.

Words: James Montgomery, 1824
Tune: CARLISLE, Charles Lockhart, 1769

The Lord's my Shepherd, I'll not want;
He makes me down to lie
In pastures green; he leadeth me
The quiet waters by.

My soul he doth restore again;
And me to walk doth make
Within the paths of righteousness,
E'en for his own name's sake.

Yea, though I walk in death's dark vale,
Yet will I fear none ill,
For thou art with me; and thy rod
And staff me comfort still.

My table thou hast furnished
In presence of my foes;
My head thou dost with oil anoint,
And my cup overflows.

Goodness and mercy all my life
Shall surely follow me:
And in God's house forevermore
My dwelling place shall be.

Words: *Scottish Psalter*, 1650
Tune: CRIMOND, Jessie Seymour Irvine, 1871

The sands of time are sinking,
The dawn of heaven breaks,
The summer morn I've sighed for,
The fair sweet morn awakes;
Dark, dark hath been the midnight,
But dayspring is at hand,
And glory, glory dwelleth
In Emmanuel's land.

The King there in his beauty
Without a veil is seen;
It were a well-spent journey
Though sev'n deaths lay between:
The Lamb with his fair army
Doth on Mount Zion stand,
And glory, glory dwelleth
In Emmanuel's land.

O Christ, he is the fountain,
The deep sweet well of love!

The streams on earth I've tasted
More deep I'll drink above:
There to an ocean fullness
His mercy doth expand,
And glory, glory dwelleth
In Emmanuel's land.

The bride eyes not her garments,
But her dear bridegroom's face,
I will not gaze at glory,
But on my King of grace;
Not at the crown he gifteth,
But on his pierced hand:
The Lamb is all the glory
Of Emmanuel's land.

Words: Anne R. Cousin, 1857
Tune: Rutherford, Chrétien Urhan, 1834

This day at thy creating Word
First o'er the earth the light was poured:
O Lord, this day upon us shine
And fill our souls with light divine.

This day the Lord for sinners slain
In might victorious rose again:
O Jesus, may we raisèd be
From death of sin to life in Thee!

This day the Holy Spirit came
With fiery tongues of cloven flame:
O Spirit, fill our hearts this day
With grace to hear and grace to pray.

O day of light and life and grace,
From earthly toil sweet resting place,
Thy hallowed hours, blest gift of love,
Give we again to God above.

All praise to God the Father be,
All praise, eternal Son, to thee,
Whom, with the Spirit, we adore
Forever and forevermore.

Words: William W. How, 1871
Tune: WINCHESTER NEW, William Monk, 1847

Triumphant Jesus bore the cross
Of cruel passion, curse, and loss;
He routed sin, and death, and woe,
And Satan my infernal foe.

Yet does the fiend still prowl and lurk,
His schemes upon my heart to work.
But God before me who can stand
When Christ in battle guides my hand?

Since Christ my Savior works within,
No more am I a slave of sin.
The hopes of hell and Satan wrecked,
No more can he charge God's elect.

No power of flesh or demon's might
Can snatch from me Christ's blood-bought right.

I more than conquer by the Word
Of Christ, my Captain and my Lord!

Words: Douglas Bond, 2007
Tune: BANFF, Paul S. Jones, 2008

◆ ◆ ◆

We rise and worship you our Lord
With grateful hearts for grace outpoured,
For you are good—O taste and see!—
Great God of mercy rich and free!

Electing love from God on high!
In gratitude I wonder why
This Sovereign Lord—O taste and see!—
In love decreed to rescue me?
Your Son obeyed the Law for me,
Then died my death upon the tree
O Jesus Christ, I taste and see,
And marvel that you purchased me!

In might, your Spirit drew me in,
My quickened heart from death to win.
O Holy Spirit—taste and see!—
From death to life you've set me free!

With thankful praise our hearts we give,
And grateful now we serve and live.
O Trinity, we taste and see
Your glorious grace so full and free!

Words: Douglas Bond, 2007
Tune: YOHO, Paul S. Jones, 2008

What wondrous love is this, O my soul, O my soul!
What wondrous love is this, O my soul!
What wondrous love is this that caused the Lord of bliss
To bear the dreadful curse for my soul, for my soul,
To bear the dreadful curse for my soul.

To God and to the Lamb, I will sing, I will sing;
To God and to the Lamb, I will sing.
To God and to the Lamb, who is the great "I AM";
While millions join the theme, I will sing, I will sing;
While millions join the theme, I will sing.

And when from death I'm free, I'll sing on, I'll sing on;
And when from death I'm free, I'll sing on.
And when from death I'm free, I'll sing and joyful be;
And through eternity, I'll sing on, I'll sing on;
And through eternity, I'll sing on.

Words: Alexander Means, 1801–53
Tune: WONDROUS LOVE, *The Southern Harmony and Musical Companion*, William Walker, 1835

When I survey the wondrous cross
On which the Prince of glory died,
My richest gain I count but loss,
And pour contempt on all my pride.

Forbid it, Lord, that I should boast,
Save in the death of Christ my God!
All the vain things that charm me most,
I sacrifice them to his blood.

See from his head, his hands, his feet,
Sorrow and love flow mingled down!
Did e'er such love and sorrow meet,
Or thorns compose so rich a crown?

Were the whole realm of nature mine,
That were a present far too small;
Love so amazing, so divine,
Demands my soul, my life, my all.

Words: Isaac Watts, 1707
Tune: HAMBURG, Gregorian chant, arranged by Lowell Mason, 1824